THE
PORTFOLIO
AND ITS USE

A Road Map for Assessment

by

Sharon MacDonald

Southern Early Childhood Association
P.O. Box 55930
Little Rock, AR 72215-5930

The Southern Early Childhood Association provides a variety of publications, videos, and
symposia for teachers and care givers of young children. For more information about our
services, write, call us at 1-800-305-7322, e-mail us at SECA@aristotle.net, or visit us on the
Internet at www.seca50.org.

SECA makes every effort to assure that developmentally appropriate practices and cultural
diversity are depicted throughout our publications, products, and materials. The opinions
expressed in this book, however, are those of the author(s) and not necessarily of SECA and/or its
affiliates.

ISBN 0-942388-20-8

Printed in the United States of America
by A.C.H. Graphics   tel. 1-501-753-6113

Contents

I dedicate this book to George—
who has been my road map.

Introduction

Several years ago I attended an assessment workshop. As the presenter spoke, I started thinking about how I assessed the children in my classroom. For some reason, assessment always meant report cards to me, and I felt that report cards, all too often, said the wrong things about children.

If I checked *not yet* or *needs improvement* under a skill column for example, I felt that I was labeling that child as *not successful*. With such labeling, families often got the message that something was wrong with their child.

I started reading everything I could to find out about alternative methods of assessment. In my search, I found substantial research that young children simply are not ready to be assessed with the traditional yardsticks of progress, so familiar in the upper grade levels.

I began to explore some alternatives. Because I was teaching in a pre-kindergarten inclusion model classroom with a co-teacher, Virginia Fleury, I had the flexibility and the encouragement from my colleague to start using the portfolio method—collecting *work samples* and writing *anecdotal records*—as an assessment tool for our preschoolers.

Work samples are specific examples of the child's work taken at regular intervals during the school year. It is important that the same category of work product be saved each time. Anecdotal records, written by the teacher, describe the child's behavior across a range of tasks and activities. The information is taken at regular intervals throughout the school year. Work samples (Chapter 3) and anecdotal records (Chapter 4) will be discussed in much greater detail later in the book.

Meanwhile back in our classroom Virginia and I wanted to collect assessment information on each child using both work samples and anecdotal records. We started very simply by collecting a few work samples and taking a few anecdotal records: one painting, one drawing, a sample of each child's handwriting (approximately every six weeks), and two anecdotal records about each child every week.

We were concerned that this type of assessment would make our jobs much harder. We were happy to learn that while our assessment work was *different*, it was not more difficult.

A real advantage was that we were able to informally record information about the children daily, rather than at a specified time in a formal manner. As we practiced, our assessments got better. It became easier to manage the amount of information and to record what we were collecting. We knew enough from past successes, and failures, to start simply. That way, we would not get so frustrated and overwhelmed that we would quit before we had given the portfolio method a fair chance of success. We knew we could add to the process over time after we developed a sound framework and an in-depth understanding of what we were doing. We knew we had started on a journey that was taking us along a new road. We knew that at the end of this journey we would be using the portfolio method to gain a clear, comprehensive picture of the children in our classroom.

We were surprised at what each portfolio told us about our children by the end of the year. The growth was tremendous and measurable. Focusing on the changes the children made provided us with a new way of looking at them. We could identify what was *successful* for each one, we could identify strengths and we could plan for the future.

It dawned on us that we were looking at the children as *they actually were*, not as we wanted them to be. We were assessing children in their natural environments in the context of their daily routines. All young children develop differently, as individuals, with unique skills and abilities. All children have different experiences along the way. Using portfolio assessment, all of the children were successful because we were measuring ongoing growth and change, rather than comparing children to some preset norm. We started seeing them as continuously acquiring different skills—or expanding their abilities—in a constant state of becoming new. We were able to ask ourselves what they were like six weeks ago, and have an answer. It was a delightful feeling to observe so much success! We were convinced we had stumbled onto something extremely worthwhile for the children, and rewarding for us.

Over the years of working with different children we have refined and expanded our approach. Now, we collect many more work samples— eight to ten different ones, every six weeks, for each child. We take more anecdotal notes for each child. We slipped, stumbled, fumbled, and met some dead ends, but at the end of the road we came up with a system that increased opportunities for success for the children, one that worked for us, and frankly, made us feel better about ourselves. Teaching is a difficult job. We often find ourselves squeezed between the expectations of administration and families and the implicit expressions of what each child needs. They often diverge.

I want to share our experience with portfolios so you can also enjoy the success of using them. Modify and adapt what you see and learn in these pages to *your* personality, *your* setting, and *your* children. Beyond the basics of the portfolio method, there is no right or absolute way to create portfolios. Give yourself time and permission to make mistakes, and to miss opportunities. Isn't that how we all learn?

Take the pressure off of yourself by focusing on the *experience* of using portfolios. Like taking a drive on a warm afternoon with no place to go in particular, you can enjoy the journey rather than worrying about getting there quickly.

Portfolio assessment is a *journey* with children; it is the observation and the recording of what they do. You are measuring their learning. Portfolios provide a new way of getting to know and to understand children. Getting started may be the most difficult part of the journey. How far you take this assessment method in your classroom depends on your own personal style. This book provides a road map. Perhaps it can be viewed as a guide not because you are lost, but because you want to travel with me to a new place. Like any journey, start at the beginning; along the way, you will enrich your experiences as a teacher of young children.

Chapter 1

How Young Children Learn

"Children learn on their feet, not on their seat!" — Margaret Puckett

In order to understand assessment, we need to look at how children acquire knowledge. Knowing how children learn will give us an understanding of why effective early childhood classrooms have a different look and function differently from the typical elementary school classroom, especially at upper grade levels. After looking at how children learn, we can continue our journey together and view assessment in terms of child interaction within the classroom environment.

Children Are Active Learners

Children naturally manipulate, smell, bend, and investigate almost everything that comes within their reach. They learn by being involved. If left alone, they follow their own natural curiosity. They are explorers, groping around unabashedly for sensory answers to their mental questions. They learn by doing!

If you find yourself being questioned about why you use these teaching methods with your children, there is help out there. An excellent resource is *Developmentally Appropriate Practice (DAP) in Early Childhood Programs Serving Children From Birth Through Age 8* (Bredekamp, 1987). It gives the documentation to substantiate what you are doing.

Under Teaching Strategies NAEYC recommends that "Teachers prepare the environment for children to learn through *active exploration* (emphasis mine) and interaction with adults, other children, and materials" (p. 54).

Children Learn by Doing Things Over and Over

Children need many opportunities to repeat activities. Materials and equipment need to be available for extended periods so that children can discover how things work. They need time also, to move from *exploring* to using the same materials and equipment for a *specific purpose*.

Figure 1. Casey uses a check-in card to help her write her name.

Figure 2. After many opportunities to write her name, Casey improved her writing.

Take a look at the photographs above. We can see two aspects of Casey's development: her writing, her painting. At first, she uses her check-in card (a sentence strip with her name on it) to help her write her name on a painting (Figure 1). Now compare this writing to the name in the bottom photograph (Figure 2). There is a vast difference. Why? Because she had many, many opportunities to write her name. While she painted during the course of several weeks, she perfected her writing skills and in addition learned about paint and the purpose of it. Casey learned by herself. She moved from exploring the properties of paint to using it with a purpose, and from exploring writing letters to making a word—her name. This was done because she wrote and she painted over and over again. It was the natural evolution of repeating or practicing a pleasurable act.

Young children enjoy practice; they can and will drill themselves. If you have ever seen children learn to tie their shoes, you know that they will tie their shoes, their neighbor's shoes, they will tie their shoes to their friend's shoes, and they will even tie their very own shoes together! Is that drill? Children will practice *all by themselves.* All they need to do is be interested and excited about what they are doing. *We* do not have to drill them. Repetition, and opportunities for repetition, are very important as children acquire new knowledge.

Children Learn Through Their Senses

If you have ever cooked food in your classroom with young children, you know how much they enjoyed the activity. This is because children learn by using their senses. They gather knowledge by seeing, smelling, hearing, feeling, and tasting. Cooking invites them to use all of the senses in understanding their experiences. Cooking is a valuable teaching tool. There are other types of activities that involve using the senses. Let's look at one.

In the fall, my class decided they wanted to adopt a tree. We toured the playground and surrounding area and voted on the tree we wanted to take care of and get to know. Doing this study of a tree involved using all of the senses except taste (although taste could have been included if the children had chosen a nut or fruit-bearing tree).

To gain knowledge about the tree, and become friends with it, I felt we had to do more than just look at the tree and give it water occasionally. We needed to really gather data about the tree. We used a telescope, a magnifying glass, a minifying glass, and our eyes to see the tree in all of its aspects, as if to say, "What is it like to be a tree? What does it do?" We used a stethoscope and our ears to listen carefully to the tree. Tree-bark rubbing and leaf rubbing involved children feeling and touching the leaves and tree trunk with their fingers and hands. We smelled the bark and the leaves and then described what we smelled. Long after the activity, the children would return to talk to the tree, to hug it, take it water, and to observe changes as one season rolled into the next. We not only learned to use our senses, but we learned first hand how to appreciate natural resources.

With each activity we use in the classroom, we need to evaluate what the children are doing. Are they using all or most of their senses? Remember, the senses are excellent channels of learning, and they are important tools for gathering knowledge.

Children Learn by Making Mistakes and Trying a Different Approach

Mistakes are an important part of learning. We want children to be willing to make mistakes! Experimenting, refining, making adjustments, and recognizing errors are essential activities if children are to learn well and retain what they learn. Through trial and error children learn how to learn and they establish learning patterns that will last a lifetime.

If they have not been discouraged from doing so, children eagerly explore the world around them. This curiosity seems largely to be built in from birth, waiting for the right developmental moments to express itself. With encouragement, children gain confidence that they can learn, and they look to themselves for answers, rather than to some external answer giver. They learn that they can problem solve. A willingness to problem solve is among the most important skills children can acquire if they are to engage in lifelong learning. The more opportunities children have to learn from trying, making mistakes, and trying again the more learning will take place.

Not too long ago, my class had a large, clear-plastic jar full of apples. The children each had predicted, and recorded, how many apples they thought were in the jar. Several children were chosen to report to the class about the accuracy of all the predictions. This team of children was given pencils and index cards to write down their findings.

This is how they solved the problem of finding out how many apples were in the jar. At first, they tried to count the apples in the closed jar. There was a big discussion about the different answers being obtained. A child suggested that they take off the lid and count the apples. They dumped the fruit on the floor. Apples rolled to all corners of the carpet area. The children tried to count them while rolling and wherever the apples stopped. Each child counted a few and when they regrouped, everyone had a different answer.

One child decided that they needed to put all the apples together to count them. So they gathered the apples in a large pile and tried

The more opportunities children have to learn from trying, making mistakes, and trying again the more learning will take place.

counting them by pointing to each one and saying a number. They kept losing track of which apples they had counted. Still they disagreed.

Finally, one of the children started lining up the apples on the carpet. They all joined in and counted the apples in the line and all agreed there were 12 apples. Their next problem was to figure out what *12* looked like and how to write it down. They each tried different markings until a child went over to the Science Center and brought back a number line. They placed each apple on a number from 1 to 12 and then copied the number 12 on an index card. Through trial and error the children found a solution to the problem.

From that day forward, the children who participated in that group activity knew how to count objects, understood how to use a number line, and could write the number 12. They worked cooperatively, without outside influence, and solved the apple-counting problem. They had learned it all through trial and error. They were willing to struggle to find the solution—to experiment with different approaches. They also learned about the value of group collaboration to solve a common problem.

Children Learn Through Modeling

In classrooms across the world teachers are mimicked by the children they teach. When a child reads a story to a group of friends, it is the same way the teacher shares a book with the children. Children model what they see and hear.

Several years ago I was unhappy with the way I taught math in my classroom. I felt so overwhelmed by all the things I was trying to do with my class that I did not think I had time to add one more thing to the curriculum. So instead of *teaching* math, I decided to model it. I put a tape measure in my back pocket and carried it wherever I went. If we were outside, I measured the length of the slide, the height of a plant, the distances between playground equipment, and whatever else I came across. In the classroom, I measured block structures, head sizes, and distances from one center to the next. Naturally, the children were curious. They wanted to measure things, too! When they questioned me, I would talk about what I was doing. We had mini-discussions about measurement.

In the Block Center, I set a basket with several tape measures. Soon the basket was empty. The tape measures were bouncing around the room in the back pockets of the children. They were measuring everything in sight. The children were doing math. As the whole class measured, I quit measuring and watched. I acquired other measurement tools and subsequently modeled their use. By the end of the year, the children had measured and quantified, in some way, almost everything in the room. They recognized the numbers on the tape measures and they had figured out that each inch was as long as a Unifix® Cube. They made charts, graphs, and recorded numbers. Modeling works!

Children Learn Through Materials and People Relevant to Their Life Experiences

For a child to learn about something, it is important to know: Is what they are learning part of his world now? Part of her daily life? Does the child relate already, and naturally, to what is being learned. Think about a child learning to tie her shoes, or learning to measure the length of a block structure. Was tying or measurement part of her daily life? Is it important, necessary, and relevant to her? She worked for hours *trying* to tie and measure. She asked, over and over again, to be shown *how* to tie and *how* to measure.

I introduced a transportation study in late October. I like to stimulate the children's interest and enthusiasm before we start a unit of study so I included them in the planning and implementation.

Down the street from school is the Bus Barn. The school district buses are parked, gassed, washed, and repaired there. Further down the street sits a wonderful little park with playground equipment, a running stream, a wooden bridge, and a hiking trail. Every other Friday we would walk past the Bus Barn to the park.

As we were sauntering by the Bus Barn on the way to the park, I talked with the children about transportation, using their familiarity with the school bus as a base of reference. I just *knew* the children were curious about buses since most of them rode a bus to school. When we walked by that Friday, I pointed out the bus and all of the activities that were going on in the Barn. The children responded with nothing other than a polite nod and a few yeas. I tried again to interest them on the return walk from the park. I asked specific questions about what they thought the workers were doing to the buses. They would have none of it!

Little point of doing a transportation study, I thought to myself, until it was important to the children. I changed my plans. Two weeks passed. I tried again. No luck. It just was not relevant to the children. I gave up any hope of doing a transportation study with the children.

In March of the following year, we were headed to the park with streamers tied to our wrist. We were in search of the wind! When we passed the Bus Barn, in unison, the children wanted to know what they were doing over there (at the Bus Barn, of course). "Why do they have that thing (a gas pump)?" asked one. "How do they wash those buses?" asked another. "Is that man fixing *our* bus...?" On and on went the questions.

I could see that interest in wind was out, buses were in, and I had better pull something together over the weekend and introduce my transportation study on Monday. When we returned to school from our walk-in-search-of-the-wind, I made a circle of knowledge with the children to see what they knew before we started (Figure 3). The circle of knowledge about transportation and buses was very simple. But, as you can see, it was a beginning. By waiting until transportation was relevant, meaningful, and important *to the children*, the transportation study was a roaring success. Note how much more information the children had acquired by the end of the study (Figure 4).

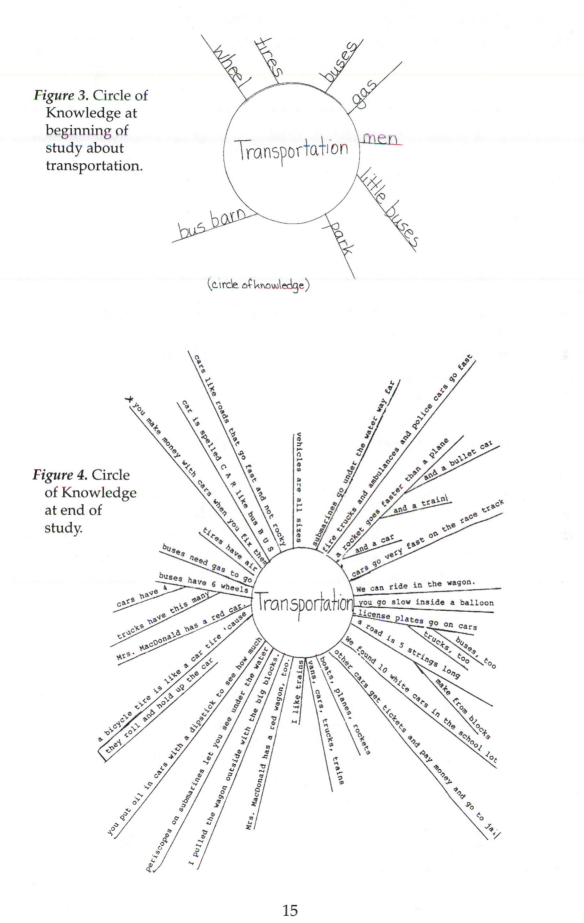

Figure 3. Circle of Knowledge at beginning of study about transportation.

Figure 4. Circle of Knowledge at end of study.

Children Learn Through Variety of Experiences

Young children need a variety of activities and materials in their classrooms because they come to group programs with different abilities and experience levels and with different developmental tasks ahead of them. Even if the children all turned five on September 1 of the same year, some children will be working at the three- or four-year-old skill level, some at the five, and still some at the six- or seven-year-old level. An inclusion program broadens the diversity of skills and abilities even more.

Because of the broad range of skills and the diverse abilities of children in any group, they need to be provided with activities on many levels. In a kindergarten Manipulative Center, for instance, have 4-, 7-, and 14-piece puzzles, as well as a large, 50-piece floor puzzle. All classroom centers or areas need materials so that all children can be successful. With encouragement, the children will move to higher levels of difficulty when they are ready developmentally, and when they are confident they can succeed. Young children succeed and move to a higher level of development in a climate of nonjudgmental acceptance.

Children have different interests and motivation, so variety is essential. Children are turned-on and tuned-in to different things. The Art Center, for example, might have a wide selection of activities such as easel and paints; drawing with markers on foil paper; dipping toy cars in paint and rolling them on paper; rubbing with dark crayons on paper over textured surfaces; drawing with crayons on sandpaper; water colors; and collage materials and bases to which the collages are attached. One of these activities will attract one child, while another activity will invite another. Variety makes the classroom experientially rich for the children.

Knowing how young children learn is reflected by how the teacher sets up the classroom. A well thought out classroom looks, feels, and functions *around the children*. Children are encouraged to make their own decisions and solve their own problems as they move around. The role of the adult is not as the dispenser of knowledge. Rather, the adult serves as the *facilitator of knowledge*. Knowledge is where the children are at the moment: engaged in their surroundings. Adults facilitate that exchange.

When a visitor who is not well-founded in early childhood education looks at a center-based classroom, she sees chaos and confusion.

She hears noise (I like to call it a creative hum). It does not look like any class she attended. It does not look like the upper grade classes she remembers well, with the order, discipline, and the children all in little rows. Because a center-based program is different, often it is necessary to prove that these programs work. We must *demonstrate* that learning is ongoing. We must be able to *document* that learning is taking place. Demonstration and documentation of learning is what portfolios are all about.

In the beginning, it was hard for me to demonstrate the success of my classroom in terms of the children's learning. There were so few pencil and paper products produced by the children. This was where portfolio assessment facilitated my understanding.

Portfolio assessment was created for center-based classrooms. Centers sometimes are called interest areas or stations. In center-based classrooms, children learn through experience in an environment prepared by the adult. The adult is not the source of knowledge. The adult facilitates the information exchanged between the child and the environment. Portfolio assessment gives teachers a way to show families, teachers, administrators, and to the community at large that children in these early childhood settings are learning, growing, and acquiring the right skills for their advancement.

Chapter 2

The Advantages of Portfolio Assessment

Portfolio assessment is a daily, on-going process in safe, comfortable, and familiar surroundings.

How are portfolios useful throughout the school year? Why should you take on a different child assessment method? How can you make time for one more thing? In other words, what are the advantages of using portfolio assessment in your classroom?

Celebrates Growth Over Time

First, through portfolios we can celebrate a child's growth and change over time. Take a look at Figure 5, Robert's handwriting samples, and consider that singular isolated events do not provide an accurate picture of success.

Figure 5. Robert's handwriting samples.

November 2, 199_

January 12, 199_

If Robert's parents came in for a conference and I showed them his attempt at writing his name in November as a singular event, they would not feel that Robert was being successful in school. On the other hand, if I showed them the writing sample from November and the January examples of Robert's writing, they probably would feel much differently. They would see two things: (1) that Robert's learning is an evolving process and, (2) that Robert is successfully learning to write. They would be celebrating Robert's success instead of focusing on his weaknesses. This approach lends itself to positive feelings. Robert feels good about himself, too, as he recognizes the progress he has made.

Happens in a Natural Setting

Portfolio assessment happens in the classroom as the child's behavior unfolds there and as he takes on tasks and activities. It is a *daily*, on-going process, in safe comfortable, and familiar surroundings.

What happens to most adults when someone says, "You will be given a test to see if you are qualified to....?" Remember taking your driver's license test? How about when the boss says, "I want that report by Monday." Adults, like children, get nervous, experience stress, and many times perform far below their potential. Children feel and perform the same way. Teachers, especially, know how it feels. When it is time for your director or your principal to evaluate your work in the classroom, and she enters your room to observe, what happens? Sweaty palms at a minimum, right! All of us fear negative evaluations by significant others. To say it another way, children would do anything to escape the critical judgment of families and/or teachers. At a time in life when children want to please others, the last thing they need is to experience failure.

Would it not be less stressful, and have far less negative impact on performance, if your director or principal entered your room frequently, and casually, throughout the year, to see what is happening. An on-going assessment over time would feel much better than a 45-minute, one-shot evaluation because it would be more realistic. When we sit a child down and say "perform," we almost always get less than the best from the child.

Helps With Planning

It was through portfolio assessment that I did a self-assessment and saw the weakness of my own math program. When I looked at each child's math skills and concepts gained over a year's time, I easily could see that it was one of my weakest areas. My report cards jumped over my deficit by giving an inaccurate assessment of the children's abilities.

Through closer observation, for example, I noticed when a child could not put together a seven-piece puzzle. I changed my method of teaching with that child immediately. Lack of success with the seven-piece puzzle told me to get out a four- or five-piece puzzle. I did not want the child to continue failing at the seven-piece puzzle when he could succeed with four pieces. *The portfolio assessment process helps drive learning and makes it possible for teachers to more adequately meet the needs of the child at the moment.* In other words, I am evaluating at the same time I am facilitating learning. Acting *now* is crucial. I do not want to wait for a formal evaluation period at the end of six weeks to record a child's failure. Not only would six weeks of trying to work the harder puzzle probably defeat her, but there would be other consequences. She no doubt would feel unsuccessful at puzzle working, and probably would not be willing to work puzzles in the future. Then, it might be too late to get out the easier puzzle.

Recently when I was writing anecdotal records during Center Time, I discovered that many of the children were talking about the characters they had seen on the television series *911*. It seemed that every notation I made around the room for several days involved some aspect of the television show. As a result of the high interest I was hearing in the classroom, I decided it was an excellent time to start a study of doctors, emergency services, police officers and fire fighters. I even watched the show to see what attracted the children so I could build on it. The change in planning came directly from my assessment of where the children's interest was at the time. On-going assessment helps drive instruction. It also helps to evaluate the overall program and its effectiveness.

Focuses on What Is Right About A Child

Often, we are so busy looking at a child's weaknesses that we forget to look at the child's strengths! We enter our classrooms with a set of preconceived ideas of where we want the children to be at the end of the day and at the end of the school year. We forget to consider that each child entering the door is different and will develop at a different rate. We need instead to look at children and find out where they are and continue from there to wherever they are able to go. This way we see what is *right* about the child. We look at what a child knows, not what the child does not know.

When my youngest child, John, entered kindergarten, he was so excited to go to real school, rather than child care, just like his brother and sister before him. He had his lunch box and his glue, his crayons, paper, and pencils. He was ready! I watched John, daily, get more discouraged and frustrated. I could not figure out where his joy, his curiosity, and his zest for knowledge had gone. I went to school for a conference with the teacher to share my concern and to see if she had any answers or suggestions. The first thing I heard was that John could not recognize his colors. I agreed. However, I never heard what John *could* do. How I wished I had heard that he could sing well and that he liked people, that he knew his whole name and he could write it backwards, and that the teacher felt he was ready to learn his colors soon.

I wanted to know what he *was* doing and where he *was* going. Being a teacher myself, I realized that she was operating from a selected set of standards that had to be mastered before any child could move to the next grade. I was able to work with her and with John to renew his joy and his interest. He regained some of both. This was a valuable lesson for me as a teacher of young children. Portfolio assessment has given me the tools I need to look at children in a *positive* way. It has given me the tools to look beyond failures and preset standards toward positive outcomes.

Gives Children an Opportunity to
Be a Part of the Assessment Process

As children take responsibility for their learning, they develop an understanding of how they can help themselves. Being part of the assessment process helps children make decisions and it allows them to own their learning. This is an important component in their development as people because joint decision making helps build self-esteem.

Children are involved in the portfolio assessment process to the degree that they are ready to participate. Three-year-olds and young fours, for example, will not have as much involvement as a five- or a six-year-old. Mostly they can look at their work, give you permission to keep it, and answer questions such as "What do you like about this (piece of work)? How is it different from this (showing them a previous sample of similar work)?" Older children can choose samples that tell something about themselves and their growth. They can answer questions such as "Why did you save this one? What does it tell you about how you have changed?"

One day I had a brief conference with Patricia about her portfolio and some of the work she had done during the year. We had the conference during Center Time. I removed from her portfolio three self-portraits for us to look at and to talk about. I placed them in front of her and asked, "Can you see how you have changed?" I was referring to how much detail she had added to her last drawing, as compared to the first two (Figure 6) She responded, pointing to the one in September with, "Yes, in this one I was just a little baby and I cried a lot. Here are the tears." Notice all the dots on her drawing. She then pointed to the one she had drawn in December and said, "This one is when I could walk and eat real food. I also know how to write my name." Notice the PRDC (for Patricia) in the upper left-hand corner of her drawing. She moved to the self-portrait she had drawn in April and said, "But in this one I am a woman, all grown up! And I have my purse to go shopping and buy everything." She was seeing her growth in an entirely different light than I was. However, both of us were focusing on her growth and her change over time. We were also looking at what Patricia could do.

Shares Information With Others

Portfolio assessment is positive proof that how we are teaching is working. It shows families, administrators, other teachers, the children themselves, and the community that the program is effective.

Parents and members of the community need to be exposed to and become educated about the value of portfolio assessment. It is expected that the validity of this new type of assessment will be challenged. As people become involved in the process, and as they develop an understanding of the value, they become supportive of this method of assessing and valuing the child.

Portfolio assessment provides useful, accurate information about each child's growth and development. Sharing this information with administrators, with other teachers, and with families brings them on to the team. Portfolios validate what we know about young children, how they learn, and how best to gather information about their developmental journey. It makes assessment part of everyday classroom experiences and it fits assessment into the daily curriculum.

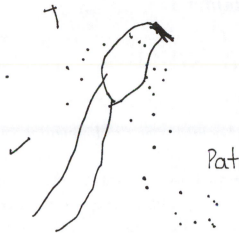

Patricia's Drawings

September 14, 199_

Figure 6. Patricia's
drawings at three
different times.

December 6, 199_

April 30, 199_

Chapter 3

Building Portfolios

Using work samples and anecdotal records to gather information gives a snapshot of each child at a particular point in her developmental course.

Many teachers already are using some elements of portfolio assessment in their classrooms. For example, if you save a few work samples on different occasions for a child, you have made a beginning. If you make notations of things that happen or if you jot down information on particular events relating to the activities of a child during the year, then you have started.

There are only two major components of the portfolio assessment process. The first is *collecting work samples* from each child. The second is *taking anecdotal records* about each child. Using both of these methods to gather information gives a snapshot of each child at a particular point in her developmental course. Accumulating them over time gives a portrait of the child's developmental progress.

Housing the Work Samples

Before you can start collecting work samples, you need to know how you will store them for future reference. Your system of saving the work needs to be in place before you start to keep track of samples gathered. If not, you will end up with a pile of papers and nowhere to put them.

There are several ways to store the children's work:
- accordion folders or pizza boxes
- X-ray folders (or manila folders rubber-banded together)
- scrap books
- three-ring binders

The following are some ideas you might use in choosing a method for housing the work samples:

1. The container needs to be divided into sections so that you have compartments for specific periods of time. The year can be divided into four-, six-, or nine-week intervals. This helps establish a framework in advance for looking at the

children's work in sequence and a time frame for doing it (that is, how often to collect materials about each child).

2. It needs to offer easy access for filing and retrieval. If children are going to be doing the filing—a very good idea for older children, the system needs to be easy for them to follow.

3. It needs to take up minimal space. Space is a prime issue in most classrooms, so the less storage space you give up, the better.

4. It needs to hold everything you want to save for an entire school year. You do not want to have more than one storage place for the work. One drawback to most containers is that you cannot save large three-dimensional items (wood constructions) or art projects (twig collages). Photograph these works and save the photographs, not the items themselves.

5. It must be inexpensive. You will be replacing the folders with each new class, so cost is a factor. In many settings you have two half-day classes, each requiring portfolio containers.

Figure 7, "Folder For Portfolios," shows how to make a pocket folder that works extremely well for accumulating children's work samples. Make as many pockets as you need. Everything fits nicely into the pockets after the child's work has been folded to fit. It does not take up much space. One *legal-size* paper box will hold 22 full folders. The cost is very low. A few hints about these folders:

1. Put the range of dates over each pocket. For example; first six weeks: August 10 through September 22. That way, you will know where to file the papers by comparing the date on the paper to the date on the pocket. This procedure helps, also, after a parent conference when the pages have all been mixed. It is easy to find where to refile them. If the children are able to file for themselves, the dates make it much easier.

2. Staple a large *laminated* index card with each child's first name in large print on the back page of the folder. Let it stick up about three inches above the folder. This makes it easy to find the file you want. Alphabetize them by their *first* name.

3. Fold paintings so the paint is inside the fold and not outside as the dried paint tends to crack and rub onto other work samples.

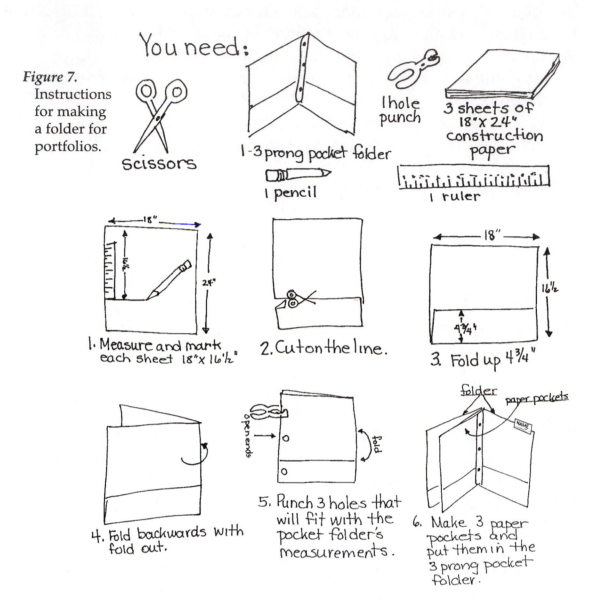

Figure 7. Instructions for making a folder for portfolios.

Consistently Keeping Track of What Is to Be Collected

To track the children's progress and growth, you will want to collect the *same* type of things many times during the year. This way you can compare the samples. First, decide what you are going to collect. Make a chart like the one shown in Figure 8. As you collect work samples for that time interval, place an X or the date in the column. Each six weeks make a new chart. Be sure to continue to collect the same information for each successive time period. You can add other things, but start with a base line of four to six work samples. These need to be on the chart each time, as well as whatever new things you want to collect. Figure 9 suggests ideas about what to collect.

Work Sample Tracking Chart

dates: from April 8 to May 22

Names	writing	Painting	Scissor	Parts	Drawing	Math	Plan B. Pgs.
A.J.	✓	✓	✓	Lib	✓	✓	4
Brittany	✓	◯	✓	Mus	✓	✓	3
Bridgette	✓	✓	✓	Comp	✓	✓	2
Clayton	✓	✓	✓	Whol	✓	✓	2
Christopher	✓	◯	✓	Comp	✓	✓	3
Casey	✓	✓	✓	D.P.	✓	✓	3
Derrick	✓	✓		Mus	✓	✓	3
Jennifer	✓		✓	Art	✓	✓	4
Jacob	✓	✓	✓	Art	✓	✓	3
Megan	✓	✓	✓	Bloc	✓	◯	2
Patricia	✓	✓	✓	Lib	✓	✓	3
Robert	✓	✓	✓	Mus	◯	✓	3
Sarah	✓	✓	✓	Mani	◯	✓	4
Justin	✓	◯	✓	D.P.	✓	✓	2
Ariel	✓	✓	✓	D.P	✓	✓	3
Cammi	✓	✓	◯	Bloc	✓	✓	3
Travis E.	✓	✓	✓	Mani	✓	✓	3
Travis T.	✓	✓	✓	Art	✓	◯	2

Figure 8. Work sample tracking chart

BUILDING PORTFOLIOS

Here are some examples of the information you may want to include in the portfolio of a young child:

Family Information
  family questionnaire
  parent's comments
  conference notes
Screening Tests and Developmental Scales
Interviews
  audio-tape recordings
  video-tape recordings
Activity Chart
Checklists
Rating Scales
Work Sampling
  copies of charts and graphs
  child's writing
  child's drawing
  child's painting
  reading and book logs
  math work
  photographs
  signs and labels
  journal pages
  plan-book pages
  scissors work
  stories (dictated or written)
  group or team projects
  notes and comment by child about their work
Anedotal Records

Figure 9. Information to include in a portfolio.

Family Information in the Portfolio

Family questionnaire

Information obtained from the family is very important. It helps you understand their perspective on their child. It helps, also, to learn about the family and what they expect from the teacher and from the school. The sample questionnaire for families (Figure 10) is included full-size in the *Portfolio Forms* section.

There are many such questionnaires that provide a similar overview. File the questionnaires in your portfolio. It helps you plan. If, for example, Johnny is fearful of dogs, you will know to make some arrangements, in consideration of Johnny's fear, before you have a dog visit school during a study of pets. Seeing how families perceive their child is a big help, too. If their view is negative, you can plan conferences to help influence a more positive attitude towards their child. If the child comes from another culture or the family has beliefs which may be affected by the activities in your classroom, responses to the parent questionnaire may alert you to these things.

Dear Parents,
Please help your child's teacher get to know your child by filling out this form. All the information will be confidential and it will be used in planning curriculum for your child's development. Please return it to school as soon as possible.
Thank you!

Child's name _____
            first   middle   last

Address _____

Nickname used by the family _____

Date of birth _____ Place of birth _____

Does your child live with: _____ both parents _____ one parent _____ other adults

   (please specify) _____

Name and ages of brothers _____

Names and ages of sisters _____

Pets (name and type of animal) _____

Does your child have a room of his/her own? _____ If not, with whom does the child

share a room? _____

Which of these best describes your child?

____ lacks self control   or   ____ uses self control

____ independent   or   ____ dependent

____ attentive   or   ____ inattentive

____ follow directions   or   ____ does not follow directions

____ confident   or   ____ shy

In what ways is your child different from other children? _____

_____

_____

What are your child's favorite play activities and interest? _____

_____

What are your child's favorite T.V. programs? _____

How many hours a day does your child watch T.V.? _____

Does your child usually play: ____ alone ____ with one friend ____ with many children

_____ with a few children _____ with older children _____ with younger children

_____ with children of the same age?

Is your child's play limited to the yard? _____ to the block? _____

Does your child attend child care? ____ from _____ to _____
                                       (times)

Into how many homes does your child go frequently? _____

Is your child enrolled in any special groups? _____

Has your child traveled out of town? ____ Where? _____

What are your child's responsibilities at home? _____

What does your child enjoy doing with the family? _____

How does your child get along with other children? _____

How does your child get along with other adults? _____

What is your biggest discipline problem? _____

_____

How do you discipline your child? _____

How do you think your child will adjust to school? _____

_____

What fears does your child have? ____ animals ____ dark ____ storms ____ strangers

other fears _____

Does your child have any nervous habits? _____

Is your child right or left handed? ____ How does your child feel about going to school?

_____

What do you hope your child will learn this year? _____

Figure 10. Sample questionaire for families.

Parent's comments

Each teacher communicates with a child's family. Some send notes while others write letters periodically or send newsletters, all in an effort to actively engage the parents in the education of their child. Whatever method used, it is helpful to relate *specific* information about what the child is doing. It is important also for the parent to have a quick and easy way to communicate with you. Save these written communications in the portfolio. Again, the information will help guide instruction for that child.

I encourage parents to review their child's work by putting a comment sheet (Figure 11) in each child's weekly take-home folder (Figure 12). The children take their week's work home in the folder. It is different from the portfolio folder. In this folder the work *not* saved in the portfolio goes home in a weekly folder each Monday and is returned empty on Tuesday, to be filled again and taken home the following Monday. This gives the parents a convenient and a specific place to make comments and return them to school. As the folder goes from school to home, and from home to school, the parent's comments, or their lack of comment, may give you a tentative view of how the parents view the child. This is helpful in creating a portrait of that child's world outside the walls of the school.

Conference notes

Whether family conferences are held at school or over the telephone, it is a good idea to keep notes. Take out the notes and review them before the next conference. What was discussed? What goals were set? What concerns expressed at the previous conference need to be looked at now? Notes taken over time give you another look at the child

Parent Comment Sheet

PARENTS: Please sign and date the comment sheet below. It helps me know you have seen your child's work. If you have any comments or questions, please use the comment space. Thank you! (Please help your child remember to return his/her folder to school.)

Date	Signature	Comments
8/21	Rita W.	It is great to see our daughter happy to go to school
8/28	Rita W. :	Is Sarah following the rules outside?
9/5	Rita W.	Thank you. Beautiful work!
9/11	Rita W.	How often do the children rotate leader?
9/18	Rita W.	Sarah is talking about her birthday. It is not until Dec. Help.
9/26	Rita W	Thank you for the conference
10/2	Rita W.	Is there a change for pictures?
10/10	Rita W.	I loved her book. It is great. Thanks.
10/16	Rita W.	Please let me know date — help Christmas
10/23	Rita W.	
11/6	Rita W.	
11/13	Rita W.	Our books are great. Thanks —
11/20	Rita W.	Sorry I forgot to return folder.
12/5	Rita W	Thanks for encouraging Sarah
12/10	Rita W	Loved the cookies.
12/18	Rita W	Merry Christmas. Thanks!

Figure 11

Take Home Folder

This is the "take home" folder. Each Monday the children take home their folder full of the work that I do not save for their portfolio. The comment sheet for the parent is stapled inside and replaced as it is filled.

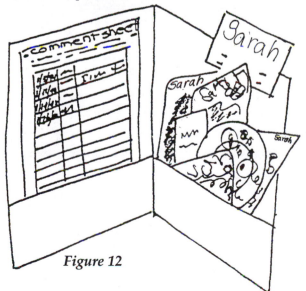

Figure 12

from the parents' perspective.

Figure 13 shows a completed "Parents Conference Notes" form that I have found useful. It is quick and easy. Notice that it focuses on the child's strengths. As you can see, we first looked at the baseline portfolio on October 7. We had no previous work to which we could compare the baseline work samples, but the parents and I discussed the portfolio process. This form works well for telephone conferences, too. For more on parent conferences, see Chapter 5.

Screening Tests and Developmental Scales

Many schools use screening tests and developmental scales to record and to measure the development of young children. Measurement instruments such as these are among the many information components of your portfolio on each child. Tests and scales are helpful in identifying skills and planning an individual educational program for each child. They are just another tool, however, in arriving at a view of the child as a whole and for planning the learning experiences that will benefit the child. The work samples and anecdotal records can give you most of the information for the scales or test so formal sit-down testing situations are rarely necessary except for diagnostic purposes. In portfolio assessment we are measuring *growth* and *development* in the child herself, not comparing her to her peers or to some other external performance standard.

Parent Conference Notes

Name of parents: Mr and Mrs. Wainstead

Name of child: Sarah   Date: 10/7

Name of teacher: S MacDonald

— After examining Sarah's portfolio —

Things the teacher would like to share: ① Sarah is eager to respond at group time. ② Sarah helps the other children find their centers. ③ She can read all the children's names. ④ She works the 50 piece floor puzzle.

Things the parents would like to share: ① Sarah talks about and plays school at home ② She likes Donny a lot ③ They feel Sarah is ready for more difficult activities and materials ④ Loved her portfolio

Things the student would like to share (if present): Sarah said she liked the home center best. She likes being Mommie. She doesn't like cleanup time.

Specific goals agreed upon by all: ① At school - I would start Sarah in Whisper Words ② at home - parents would take her to the library more often. ③ wanted to see portfolio growth again in Dec.

Figure 13. Form to record conference notes.

Interviews

Audiotape recordings

One of the most effective ways of gathering information about oral language development in young children is by using cassette-tape recordings. While it is time consuming, it is worth it, since you get a clean, audio snapshot of the child's growth and change. Three times a year is ideal; at the beginning, at the end, and sometime in the middle. If you only can get a recorded sample twice, the beginning and end are the obvious choices. The main focus of audio recording is language development. In addition, other attributes of the child appear during the audio interview that are very useful in assessment:

- the child's thought processes
- planning skills
- ability to attend to a subject for a reasonable time period

To get the best response at the beginning of the year, wait several weeks before you begin. This gives the children time to feel comfortable in the school setting.

Here are several questions I like to ask in a child's interview (choose the ones that fit your setting and your needs):

1. What do you like about school?
2. Where do you like to play the most?
3. Who do you like to play with in the _____ Center?
4. Would you like to sing a song? (If they have trouble thinking of one, I usually suggest one that is familiar.)
5. Would you like to tell a story? (I usually suggest one that is familiar.)
6. What can you tell me about the number 3? 10?
7. Why do you think you come to school?
8. Tell me about _____ (show them an object: a toy, a tool, a rock or something that may be unfamiliar to them.)

If you see the child losing interest during the interview, stop the tape. (Note: I have never been able to keep a child focused for longer than 5 to 10 minutes. It might take two interviews to complete an audio interview.)

When you have finished the tape, *be sure to let the children listen to themselves.* Again, this involves them in the process of their own education and allows them to add something else to it.

Videotape recordings

Videotaping children is more expensive than audio taping, but you get so much more information. If you can ask each parent to send a blank VCR tape for their child, and if you have access to a camera, you have an excellent way to get a more complete portrait of the child's development at that point. Video each child for 15 minutes while she is at play, while she is dramatizing a story, dancing, swinging or working a problem with a friend. This can be done two or three times a year, just like the audiotaping. Videotape is an excellent assessment tool to have in the portfolio.

Activity Chart

Sometimes we do not know where a child spends his time in the classroom, moving from one center, or area, to another. We might feel he is spending too much time doing one thing only, but we really are not sure. To validate your impression, use an activity chart. The activity chart gives you a record of the child's movement and interest through the day. Often, typically at the beginning of the school year, a child will be fearful to leave a particular area and move to another. When you find out by using the activity chart, you can encourage the child to select another area, and ease him through the transition.

By using the activity chart you also might see that a child is choosing an area because of a high interest level. If that is the case, take advantage of the child's interest by having a broad range of skills and concepts available for her exploration and use. For example, if you are working on shapes, and the child chooses the Block Center every day, add shaped, paper props to the center or add some block activities that require making shapes with blocks like a square, a rectangle, a triangle, and a circle.

Figure 14 shows that John spent much of his time in the Manipulative Center at the first of the school year. John was quiet and withdrawn. I wanted to track his movement through the classroom for my own information, and I wanted to have documentation about John's center selection and interest to share with his parents. By my knowing that John played only in the Manipulative Center, I was able to encourage him to explore the other areas in the classroom. Gradually he felt more comfortable and he was able to get involved in other constructive activities. I kept track of his movement three times during September, October, and November (as you can see in Figure 14). I did it on one sheet rather than on three sheets. This helped me see his different movements through the classroom on seperate recording days.

Checklists

A variety of checklists are available for purchase; many, on the other hand, can be made by the teacher. The major advantage of a checklist is that it is quick and easy to administer. The major disadvantage is that it does not describe the quality of the children's work. Because of this, getting an accurate developmental portrait of the child is sometimes difficult with a checklist.

For example, my class planted pumpkin seeds and two weeks later we saw a few sprouts. Sarah, whose interest was high, was working with pumpkin sequence cards. There were four cards: the first showed the pumpkin seed; the second, a mound of soil where the seed had been planted; the third, the soil being watered; and the fourth, the plant sprouting from the soil. I had an entry line on the checklist that read "Four-sequence Mastery." I watched as she put the cards in the correct order, except she placed the mound of earth last in the sequence. I felt that Sarah knew the sequence, but I marked "Developing" on the Four-sequence Mastery entry line. A few minutes later I was passing-by again. I heard Sarah tell her friend, Patricia "This is my pumpkin plant. I planted it. I watered it. It grew! It died, and I threw it away!" The order Sarah used was not the one I had anticipated, but it was a sequence of four cards and it told Sarah's story and her comments revealed her mastery. I quickly scratched my "Developing" entry, and I replaced it with the word "Mastered."

Figure 14. Daily activity chart for a child.

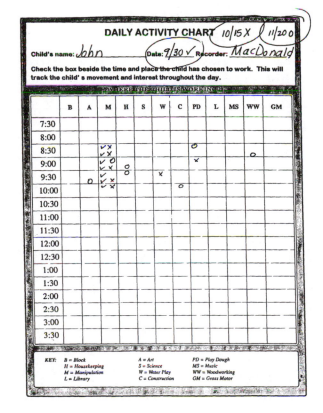

The lesson for me was that there are *some* skills that can be assessed with a yes or no answers, but because of the way checklist questions are asked, we can miss the experience that Sarah had, one that revealed her accomplishment of an important developmental task. Checklists are useful but, just like any other assessment device, important developmental events can be missed if checklists are relied upon exclusively.

Checklists, however, are an important tool for the portfolio process. Virginia and I were given a computer and a printer for our Pre-K class. Several programs were included that were suited for our children. We were concerned about how best to use the computer, how to take care of it, and how much to allow the children to use it. After a lot of thought we came up with a checklist. We wanted to know how much the children knew about using computers and how much skill they already possessed. It helped us focus on what skills were needed to use the computer without damaging it. After assessing each child we were able to give much more freedom to some children, but less to others, and we identified the children who needed teacher or peer tutoring before they could begin (Figure 15).

Other types of checklists look at different skills and concepts. Many school settings use a developmental checklist as the heart of their portfolio. They gather work samples and anecdotal records to document mastery of the developmental skills. The developmental checklist is used as a reporting device to parents. Some possibilities are included in *Portfolio Forms*.

Rating Scales

A rating scale measures one particular capability or behavior. If you think, for example, that a child is having difficulty listening to a story in a whole group setting, you might use a rating scale to assess if you are right. The rating scale requires planning and time to observe the child. I have used it to find out if a child can follow a multi-step direction (see the top of Figure 16). As you can see, in November Casey could do a two-step direction easily, but she was unsuccessful at a three-step instruction. Later, she could follow a three-step direction fairly well and by April, she was on-track developmentally. The bottom rating scale in Figure 16 evaluates how well Casey listens to a story in a large group. In September, it was hard for her to focus with so many distractions. At that time, she could attend in a small group but by January, she was able to focus on the storyteller in the large group, and to follow and enjoy the story in large group.

The following are a few behaviors or capabilities that you might use to assess a child by using a rating scale:

1. Does the child participate orally in a whole group setting?
2. Does he sing a song from beginning to end?
3. Does she display leadership qualities in a group or team situation?
4. Does he share materials?
5. Can she retell a story to others?

COMPUTER SKILLS CHECKLIST

NAME _Jacob_

+ signifies that the child can do the task - signifies that the child cannot do the task	baseline 1	update 2	update 3	update 4	update 5	update 6
DATE	10/2	11/30	/10	2/30	3/26	4/13
watches screen	+					
uses track ball or mouse to move arrow	+					
moves arrow to specified place using track ball or mouse	+					
matches letters using the trackball or mouse	−	+				
uses keyboard to access the screen	−	+				
matches letters using the keyboard	−	−	+			
draws with the mouse or trackball	−	−	−	+		
fills in spaces with the mouse or trackball	−	−	−	+		
erases with the mouse or trackball	−	−	−	+		
chooses activity using program menu	−	−	−	−	+	
uses menu to access program of choice	−	−	−	−	+	
uses keyboard to write letters, words, or numbers	−	−	−	−	−	+
matches the printout with the screen	−	−	−	−	−	+

This checklist was created by *Virginia Fleury and Sharon MacDonald*

Figure 15. Computer skills checklist.

Work Sampling

Set up deadlines to collect a child's work five or six times during the year. I collect in six-week blocks of time. Read through each description of work you might collect, then decide which you can collect

Rating Scale

Child's name _Casey_

Key: 1. needs more time
2. satisfactory
3. excellent

Behavior: _multi-step directions_	Date	Rate
2 steps - Go shelf - take book	11/93	2
3 steps - water plants	12/93	1
3 steps - art activity	1/94	2
3 steps - props for song	4/94	3

(comments)

Figure 16. Two rating scales for Casey.

Rating Scale

Child's name _Casey_

Key: 1. needs more time
2. satisfactory
3. excellent

Behavior: _attends to story_	Date	Rate
Brown Bear - whole group	9/93	1
Little Red Hen - small group	11/93	3
Bread Bread Bread whole group	12/1	2
Gunny Wolfe - whole group	1/94	3

(comments)

over time and which you can gather randomly. Choose three to four work products to collect if you are just beginning to use portfolios and six or seven if you are more experienced. The items you decide to collect consistently over the year will create a baseline from which growth and change can be assessed. For example, each six weeks I collect the following and they become my baseline products:

- a writing sample
- a painting
- scissors work
- a self-portrait
- a math sample
- three pages of a child's plan book
- a photo of the child involved in an activity

Other things are saved as they occur. At the end of the school year I have six work samples of the baseline materials. Many of the following types of samples lend themselves well to creating a baseline, and others are better gathered spontaneously, as they occur.

Copies of charts and graphs

Any chart or graph where a child's work is noted can be copied and placed in the child's portfolio. There are many graphing or charting activities that easily can be added to the portfolio. It is important that the individual child's contributions are documented. This takes a little more time at the beginning, but it gives you valuable information about the child and about your teaching.

The Apple Graph in Figure 17 is an example of a graph that was helpful in looking at two skills relating to each child in the classroom.

At the time the children were participating in a study about apples as a group. They tasted a slice of each variety of apple: a green apple, a red apple, and a yellow apple. I displayed the blank graph on the tray. Beside the graph I placed three small baskets and a glue stick. In each basket there were three baskets of paper apples: red, yellow and green. Each set had written on it each child's name. The children could choose the color of apples they liked the best and, at the same time, find the one on which I had printed their name.

The leader, Justin, demonstrated how this worked. First, he decided which apple flavor (and corresponding color) he liked best. His choice was red. Justin found the red paper apple on which his name was written. Next, he used the glue stick and applied glue to the back of the paper apple. Last, he put his apple on the "1" row, just above the "Red" column (see Figure 17).

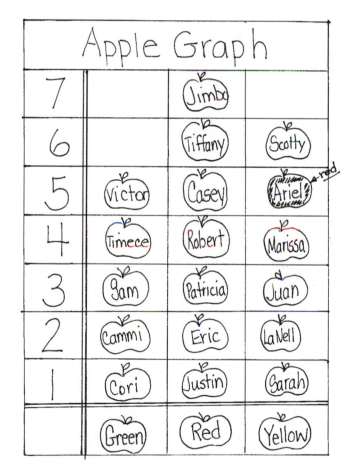

Figure 17. Apple graph.

After the children understood the instructions, I moved the activity and the graph to the Science Center. The children were responsible for going to the center during the day, remembering their favorite apple, finding it with their name, and placing it in the correct box on the Apple Graph.

This activity was multistep and many skills had to have been mastered and used by the children to accomplish it. There were several things I learned about the children working at this activity. First, most of the children were able to accomplish a multistep task. One child, Ariel, however, had placed the red-paper apple in the yellow column (see Figure 17). Second, most of the children were able to complete the task independently. Third, the children could match colors. Fourth, I knew they all recognized their names. Fifth, and last, they understood the concept of simple graphing. I knew that the class was ready to move on to more complicated graphing. I knew, also, that I needed to work with Ariel to do graphing in a simpler form. At the end of the activity, I copied and reduced the graph and made copies for each child's portfolio.

The apple drying science experiment shown on the Daily Activity Chart, Figure 18, is another example of data gathering from a whole-group activity. The children had previously dried an ear of corn so the following experience was not new to them. They had sliced apples and threaded the apple slices on a four-foot long piece of string. I listed each child's name on a chart. I asked each child to tell me what they thought would happen to the apple slices when I stretched them across the window and tied them to nails at the window edge (to dry). You can see the children's predictions in Figure 18. After their predic-

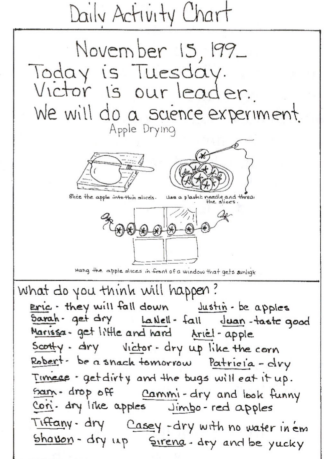

Figure 18. Daily activity chart for apple drying experiment.

tions were made, the children had to wait for the results of the experiment. I transferred the information to a small sheet of paper and made copies for each child's portfolio. From the experiment, I learned which children understood the previous "drying" process involving the corn, and which children could "transfer" (apply) that knowledge from the corn to the apple-drying activity. I gained an insight into their thinking skills. I could see that the activity was too open-ended for some of the children. Their responses not only helped me look at the children individually, but I was able to adjust my expectations for many of them prior to beginning a new activity—drying a pumpkin.

Writing

When children begin to write, they scribble. They scribble all over everything, as you probably have noticed. Later they develop more control. Their scribbles become tighter, and they begin to make mock letters (letter approximations). Mock letters look like they could be letters if you could just rotate them in one direction or the other. Later they start to make letters that actually look like the real ones, but they are placed randomly around the page. They are not put together for a particular purpose, like a word. These letters are the spontaneous expressions of children's play with images in their heads. They can read them to you, if you ask or, even better, read you the story they tell! Gradually, children begin to use invented spelling with consonants, and start putting spaces between words. They read invented words the same way, over and over again. This entire process marks the beginning of written communication. It is a very exciting time for children and for their adults, and it is especially worth tracking during the year.

Each child moves through the developmental stages of writing at a different rate. It is important to keep a record of their progress. Your expectations can be adjusted based upon your assessment of children's growth at particular points in time. If a child has good hand-finger control with a pencil, for example, and grip pressure that suits him, he is ready to fine-tune his writing. On the other hand, if his letter formation is primitive, it tells you that you need to give him more time and more meaningful opportunities to write. It is important to give these opportunities when the desire and motivation are present.

The point is, you begin to acquire information about how to shape your instruction to the needs of individual children, and **they tell you through their actions when to do it**. Writing samples give you information about each child, and that information must be built into the curriculum. Remember what was said earlier in this book: **evaluation through the portfolio process drives curriculum**. In other words, how children respond to activities determines what activities and materials are offered next.

Look at the changes that took place in Cammi's writing (Figure 19). By April, she had gained control over her fingers. She had grasped that the individual letters in her name form the word *Cammi*, with unique sound and a unique shape to each letter. In the example, Cammi moves with her hand just like she reads: from the left to the right. She has developed from writing approximations of words to the words themselves.

There is an excellent chart that shows the stages of emergent writing in *Developmentally Appropriate Assessment* (Shores, 1995).

Drawing

A child's drawings are like looking through windows into her mind and her experiences. If you look, for example, at Marissa's three drawings acquired throughout the year (Figure 20) you can see that she started in October at the *tadpole* stage of drawing in

Figure 19. Cammi's writing samples.

rendering her own portrait. She did not exactly plan it ahead of time, but built one element upon the other. Three months later she added more parts to her body. She was better organized in approaching the task. She started with the head and moved downward to the rest of her body. In the third drawing in April, because she had gained knowledge and control from previous experiences, she was able to plan her drawing and to add even more body parts. She evolved from a scribble-like rendering to an actual self-portrait. This gives us a perspective of her growth and development that we cannot get in any other medium.

Painting

Gather samples of children's painting at regular intervals during the year. The developmental stages through which children pass bring them to the point at about age 5 or 6 of being able to paint likenesses,

Figure 20.
Marissa's self-portrait drawings.

or representations, of the things they see. They can go to the easel and capture the likeness, or essence, of what they have chosen to paint. At this developmental point, painting represents something very valuable to the child. Casey's painting progress through the year is documented through Figure 21. In these illustrations, I am presenting more paintings than I typically keep for portfolios because they document a more detailed progression of the incremental changes in Casey's work over time. Her progress is compressed over a shorter time than for most children, perhaps because she had never painted before.

Figure 21a: In September, Casey explored the medium. She was discovering the properties of the paint and of the brushes. She covered the page with the various colors to explore the materials. She did this for one month, painting daily.

Figure 21a

Figure 21b: Casey discovered she could control the paint and make lines. She made vertical lines across the page. She started painting purposefully. She developed a beginning understanding of patterns. She created line, space, line, space, line—the beginning of an AB pattern. She also was fairly consistent with the sizes of the lines, showing she had gained more control over the brush and the paint.

Figure 21c: Casey has moved to a different developmental stage. She did not plan to make a heart, but it occurred spontaneously (discovery) and then she drew several more on the page after her discovery. After this event, she made hearts on every painting for weeks. She would say before she went to the easel, "I am going to paint hearts!"

Figure 21d: Casey has moved into a more controlled stage. She has made a rainbow. It is a recognizable form. Also she has made a pat-

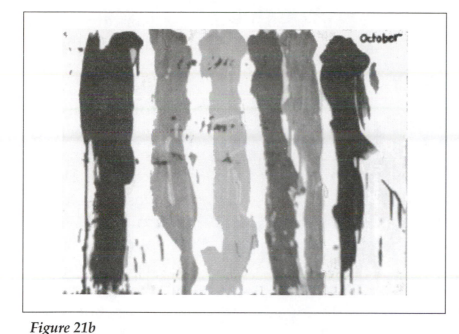

Figure 21b

tern of curved stripes. She has definitely gained control of the brush and more control over the paint. Each painting is more symbolic than random experimentation.

Figure 21e: This is the first of many of self-portraits. Casey, still in the *tadpole* stage, has her arms and legs coming from her head (or her body). She added hair. When she was telling me about the picture she said, "I have golden curls all over because my Mama rolled up my hair with her rollers. They were hot, but I am beautiful!"

Figure 21f: From this point on, Casey went to the easel with a plan of what she was going to paint. Sometimes she followed through with her plan, and other times she did not. We had been discussing a but-

terfly we had seen on the playground, when she decided that she would paint it so we could remember it. She went to the easel and painted the butterfly. With this rendering, she moved to the *representational* stage of

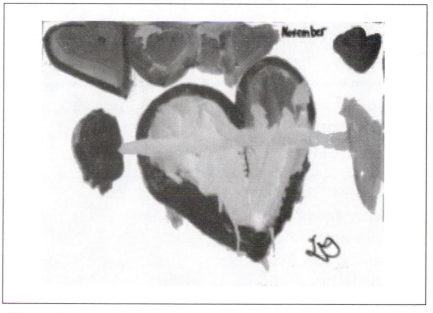

Figure 21c

Figure 21d

painting—painting the butterfly in her head to stand for the real one we had seen on the playground.

Figure 21g: Casey is still painting self-portraits. She has moved from the *tadpole* stage, but is not yet fully representational. She has added a body to her head, and she has arms with the beginning representation of fingers. The arms are placed on the body in the correct position.

Figure 21h: Casey goes to the easel with a purpose. She has become quite adept at painting a self-portrait. She now has fingers and shoes. She added clothes with buttons. She has things pretty much in proportion, and she has the body parts in the right places. Casey's use of colors and the increased size of her work suggests a new self-confidence.

Figure 21i: The last painting shows that Casey has moved into another stage of development. She has a horizon line in her painting. The grass is below

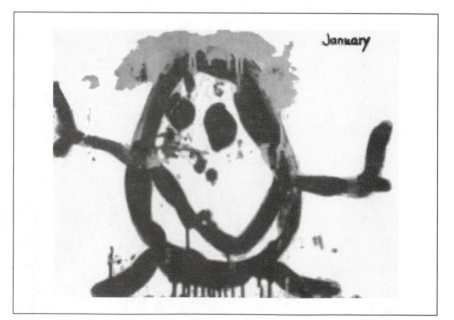

Figure 21e

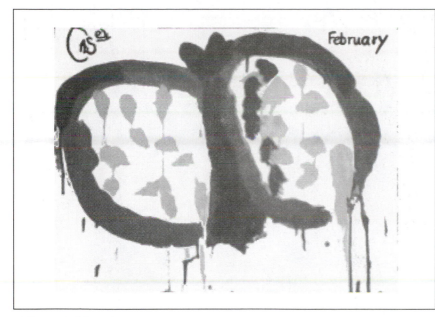

Figure 21f

the house and the sun is above in the sky. She went to the easel with the expressed purpose of creating a painting that represents her "new" bicycle. Casey is developing a sense of scale in her object relationships. She is using proportion and perspective.

We get so much information about growth and change from children's paintings. Our principal goal in encouraging painting is to make it possible for them to grasp that **symbols can stand for the objects, places, and the things they see around them.** When they understand symbolic meaning, they can learn that letters represent things, like sound, and as they begin to learn letters, they can learn words. They can comprehend that a plastic apple can represent a real apple and that other models, like a red ball, can represent different things. They can learn that numbers represent a group of objects, and so on. The understanding that

Figure 21g

symbols such as numbers and letters can represent things is an essential concept for young children to learn. You can find out if children are using representational thinking by looking at their paintings. This knowledge drives your curriculum planning.

Figure 21h

Note: To make the storage of paintings in portfolios easier, and less messy, after the paintings have dried, fold them, painted surface facing inside, and put the child's name and date on the outside. This makes them much easier to file, and the paint will not rub off on other work.

Reading and book logs

Children's early reading skills can be documented in several ways. When a child retells a story, you know she has heard and processed the story information. She understood the story sequence. This developmental achievement is predictive of the capacity for further reading skills.

When a child collects and reads labels, signs, wrappings, and packaging materials, you have documented proof that he has begun the reading process. When a child writes a story in a blank booklet, and then reads it to you, you can see if she moves left to right and top to bottom. You can see if she has an awareness of the story process (an introduction, an immersion in a time and a place, characters, events, and a resolution or ending). Sometimes a child will just label pages, leaving the page otherwise blank. If a child reads his story and it is disjointed and non-sequential, he has not developed to the point of understanding the story process. More time and practice are needed.

In my classroom I have an *informal* reading program called "Whis-

Figure 21i

per Words." Each child has 5" x 8" index cards and a large envelope. They can whisper to me a word they want to learn to read. I write the word on the index card, and they read it. The envelopes stay in a basket in the Library Center, so at anytime they can read their words to a friend or read their friends' words. "Whisper Words" allow children to make choices and honors those choices. If I have many children who choose not to learn any other word than their name, it is okay. There is time.

A copy of children's reading vocabularies are kept in their portfolios. Usually, children begin with names of people important to them and with other nouns. When they are ready, they add verbs. Some words that children want to use first include

- wants
- loves
- likes
- feels

It is fun to watch them use verbs. These first verbal steps seem to infuse in them a sense of mastery. The verbs also enable them to form sentences. "Sarah likes Barney" was a sentence one child created from his whisper words.

Reading logs are used when children become more fluent readers, to keep track of what they read. In upper grades for example, logs can be reviewed and summarized by the student and the teacher to document reading activity. The same idea can be used earlier with some modifications. Document the books you read to the class by making a reading log that can be copied and placed in a portfolio. Ask parents to keep a log of the books they have read to their child. This can be taken a step further by having a child evaluate the story that was read to him at home or at school (Figure 22). In this figure, you can see the list of books we read during our study about winter. As we read the books, we created our log and evaluated our stories. At the end of the page we voted on our favorite story. *Frosty* won! I made copies of our logs and put a copy in each child's portfolio.

Math work

There are many ways to record math development. Look for papers and drawings the children create spontaneously in their daily activities that relate to math and to their understanding of mathematical processes. Let's look at three examples.

Reading Log

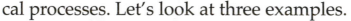

Title	Liked	Did Not Like
Round Robin	☺	☹
The Snow Child	☺	☹
White Snow, Bright Snow	☺	☹
Red Mittens	☺	☹
Snowy Day	☺	☹
The Mitten	☺	☹
The Tomten	☺	☹
Frosty	☺	☹

Figure 22. Reading log with children's evaluations.

Figure 23 depicts a score sheet for a game Clayton and Travis played called The Peanut Drop. The object of the game was to see who could drop the most peanuts into a small plastic jar placed in the bottom of a larger one. They had to use tongs to pick up and to drop the peanuts into the jar. These boys created their own score sheet. They drew a box and wrote their names. As they dropped a peanut in the smaller jar they put a check mark for their respective side on the score sheet. As you can see, Travis was ahead 6 to 3. Clayton got a little frustrated losing and scribbled on the page; then he lost interest

Clayton and Travis —
Keeping score for peanut drop.

Figure 23

48

and left. At that point, the game was over. Travis sat down with the paper and carefully counted each side and wrote the total for himself and for Travis at the bottom of the page. He then taped it to the wall above the game. From that time forward, I had a whole class of children keeping score on The Peanut Drop. I saved the results for each child and placed them in their portfolio.

Figure 24 shows the result of LaNay's counting the number of fall leaves she had collected on her fall walk. LaNay could not find the number line in the classroom, so she improvised and made her own. Notice that *6* and *9* are missing. After she made the number line, she placed her leaves on each number, and she counted. She actually had seven leaves, but the count showed eight on her number line. I saved her number line because *she understood the concept of a number line* and how to use it. LaNay could count to 23 and she could recognize numbers from the classroom number line, so I was not concerned that she could not yet *write* all the numbers.

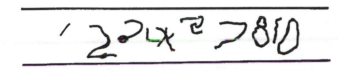

Number line
(for counting leaves)

Figure 24

Figure 25 shows another example of an event that led to my including a child's work in his portfolio. Typically, I keep graph paper in the Science Center for those occasions when graphing fits into other activities the children are doing. If we have created a graph as a group, the children have graph paper available to duplicate the group's efforts or in case they want to graph something else. Often, they get spontaneous and surprising ideas. One day, (see Figure 25) Michael made his own graph evidently because there was no more graph paper in the Science Center. He had a pocket full of rocks when he came in from the play-

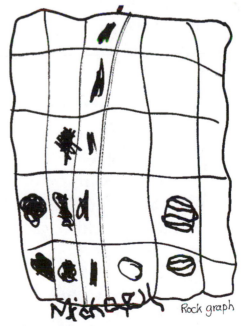

Rock graph

Figure 25

ground. First Michael graphed the rocks themselves on a large graph. Next he drew his own graph, and he represented each shape of rock with rock-shaped marks. This was a big step. He knew *how to make representations* of his rocks. Notice that the drawings in each column on the graph are different. He worked from the bottom but he had one more thin rock than he had spaces. I put this paper in his portfolio to show his understanding of graphing.

These are just a few examples. Look at the math-related activities you do in your classroom and find the ones that provide a view of the child that has not been documented in other ways.

Photographs

Sometimes it seems that children develop so very slowly. I think it is because we are with them every day and the growth is not seen when observed in one-day time intervals. On the other hand, when we look at photographs taken with reasonable time periods between, the growth and change become clear. We become more encouraged that our efforts are worthwhile. Photographs are wonderful ways to assess young children as they progress. Here are several ways to use them.

Let parents know what you are doing by using photographs. Send them home with the child. Take a look at Joshua at the easel in Figure 26. The report is really a form-and-photograph combined that I use often to show children working in differ-

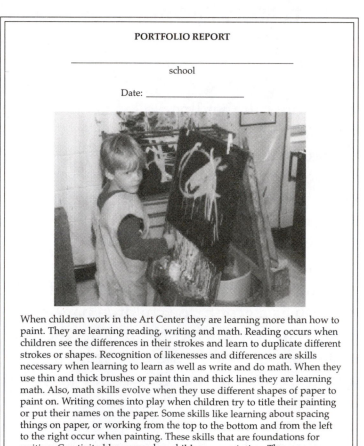

PORTFOLIO REPORT

_____
school

Date: _____

When children work in the Art Center they are learning more than how to paint. They are learning reading, writing and math. Reading occurs when children see the differences in their strokes and learn to duplicate different strokes or shapes. Recognition of likenesses and differences are skills necessary when learning to learn as well as write and do math. When they use thin and thick brushes or paint thin and thick lines they are learning math. Also, math skills evolve when they use different shapes of paper to paint on. Writing comes into play when children try to title their painting or put their names on the paper. Some skills like learning about spacing things on paper, or working from the top to the bottom and from the left to the right occur when painting. These skills that are foundations for writing. Creativity blossoms when children are painting. There are many ways to put the paint on the paper and many ways to express ideas and thoughts. Expressing creativity leads into building problem solving skills.

Figure 26. Portfolio Report for Joshua.

ent centers in the classroom. The words are general; specific information is provided by the photograph. It shows families their own child in action. The reason I prepare these reports is so the parents can see how their child learns and can come to value the process taking place. I send home a photograph every six weeks describing what takes place in each center. When the photographs are accumulated over time they also show the child growing and changing. These reports help parents understand that a young child learns:

- through play
- by doing things over and over
- by trial and error

stack and row

enclosures

Figure 27. Photos of Justin in the Block Center, revealing his developments.

Another way to use photographs is to show children as they move through the developmental stages of block building (Figures 27). In January, Justin was in the ***building begins*** phase of his development, building vertically and horizontally, placing blocks in stacks and rows. In March you see him evolve in his ability to use and to build with blocks. He has learned about inside and outside. Building *enclosures* is the precursor to ***representational building***, an important stage for block building in that it lays the foundation for accepting representations, or likenesses, of things— the beginnings of abstract thought. Knowing how far along Justin is in his block-play development suggests where his next step along the continuum would be (Figure 28). This awareness helps us know how to facilitate his learning.

Stages of Block Play

Stage 1. **TOTE AND CARRY:** Blocks are carried around to feel their smoothness, to see how heavy they are and to hear what kind of sounds they make when they fall. Children like to fill containers, dump them out, and refill them. (2 to 3)

Stage 2. **BUILDING BEGINS:** Children lay the blocks on the floor in rows, either horizontally or vertically with much repetition. Children may play alone or near other children, but rarely in a cooperative way. (3)

Stage 3. **TRIAL AND ERROR BRIDGING:** Two blocks with a space between them, connected by a third block. Children learn to bridge by trial and error. (3 to 4)

Stage 4. **ENCLOSURES:** Blocks are placed in such a way that they enclose a space. Bridging and enclosing are among the earliest "technical" building problems that children have to solve. As children work at building enclosures, they learn the spatial concept of inside and outside. (4)

Stage 5. **REPRESENTATIONAL BUILDING:** At this stage, 4- and 5-year-olds add dramatic play to their block building. They name their structures which relate to a function. Before this, children may also have named their structures, but the names are not necessarily related to the function of the building.

Stage 6. **BUILDING SOCIODRAMAS:** By age 5, group cooperative play is common. Children decide beforehand what they want to build, and they may reproduce structures that are familiar to them. Children may ask to leave their structure standing and may play with it again.

Figure 28. Stages of block play.

Photographs also can be used to document children in their emergent stages of reading. In Figure 29 you see Michael using early reading behaviors. He was an emergent reader at this point. Photographs and notes of explanation are important and useful tools for providing information for me and to the families.

Signs and labels

Young children like to label things. They seem to look for any reason to label and apply signs to objects. I think that it helps them gain a sense of mastery of the settings in which they find themselves and of the skills they are acquiring. These signs and labels provide valuable information about their writing development, their understanding that word groups convey messages, and their ability to build on prior knowledge.

Figure 29. Michael reading.

Emergent reading behavior
turns pages left to right
spends time on each page
moves eyes left to right

Starting to enjoy stories
smiles at pictures that are funny
shows friends significant pictures
makes appropriate facial expressions

Retells familiar story

Here are three examples:

The top of Figure 30 shows Eric's sign from the Block Center saying, "Do not knock my building down." He was leaving the center for a few minutes and he wanted to protect his building. He realized that he couldn't tell everyone in the class orally but he could get the message across to them by writing a sign. Other children wanted to read Eric's sign because they were curious about what he had to say. The sign also tells a lot about his writing development. I saved it for his portfolio.

Figure 30 (bottom) shows the label Robert placed on a block structure: "This is the three little pigs house." We had read several

Figure 30. Signs and labels from the Block Center.

versions of the *Three Little Pigs* and dramatized the story. Cognitively, Robert was extending his knowledge from the format, *The Three Little Pigs* (and their houses) to another format, by building *his* version of the three little pigs' house.

The written cover of Edward's research project on worms and photographs of his work on the project are shown in Figures 31 and 32. We had filled the water table with sand and bait worms. We posted instructions and signs on the wall to show the children what to do. Edward was able to follow the signs and read the instructions.

All three of these examples demonstrate how children's mastery of language can be documented in their portfolios.

Journal pages

Many teachers use journals to encourage children to write and to express themselves through writing. There are many kinds of journals. Some formats are structured, such as asking children to copy parts of the daily chart. Other journals are open-ended, when children write on any subject they choose. The journal pages depicting changes

record
Look
Worms
Touch

EdWard

Figure 31. Edward's worm
research paper.

Figure 32. Edward's research.

in children over time need to
be photocopied and placed in
their portfolios. These records
are an excellent source of information especially about writing
skills and mental development.

Plan books

Plan books are similar to
journals but they have a more
specific purpose—for children to
plan their day. When the children write their plans, they do
so on paper already prepared
and placed in a three-pronged folder. I have written the date across the
top. Across the top half of the paper, I ask children to write down

1. what they plan to do that day
2. to think about to what center(s) they are going
3. to say what they are going to do there
4. to say with whom they will work

5. to identify what tools they will need to work there

The information in a plan book can be scribbling, lines, words, letters, or drawings. Later in the day, children come back to the whole group and write a review of what they did. I ask questions such as:

- Did you go where you said you would go?
- (If not) Why not?
- Did you play with the person(s) you planned to play with?
- Did you work at the things you said?

These questions help children reflect on their center time and review their actions compared to their plan. A page of Megan's plan book appears in Figure 33. She drew herself going to the Motor Lab (you can see the "MOT" in the upper left quadrant of her plan). She did not get to go there this day

Figure 33

so she wrote "No" at the bottom in her review. In Figure 34, you can see she has developed many skills in writing and drawing from January to April. She decided she was going to the Home Center, planned to play with Janel, and she was going to be Snow White. When she reviewed her time at the center, she did what she said she was going to do, following her plan. Children benefit from being responsible for their time and from the experience of expecting to be responsible for themselves. In time, expecting to be responsible becomes part of their routine and their learning is moved further along.

Figure 34. Megan's April plan / review.

These examples of Megan's work told me she was able to follow a plan. Megan thought specifically about what she was going to do, how she was going to do it, and then followed through by doing it.

Scissors work

To document fine motor development, I save examples of children's cutting activities. When a child cuts pictures from magazines, for example, I will date one of the pictures and put it in his portfolio. At the end of the year, it is interesting to see how his fine motor skills have developed in that his cut-lines become less jagged, more fine, and lines traverse a straighter line.

Group or team projects

There are many opportunities to document children working together in groups of two or more. You can focus on cooperation, sharing, taking turns, or peer tutoring. Finding ways to document these social skills sometimes is not easy. I like to do many team activities. Here are two activity examples to give you an idea of what you can do to acquire the necessary developmental information.

We were going to the zoo. The children predicted which animals they thought they would see. I found pictures of the animals and reproduced their shapes on a research checklist for the children [Figure 35 (right)].

In the first project, each pair of children was given a different color crayon with their checklist. As we walked through the zoo, the children worked in teams to color the boxes next to animal shapes on the checklist. When we returned from the zoo, the sheets told me which children worked well in groups. I could look at the child pairs and see who understood the project, if the children took turns coloring the little boxes indicating each of the animals as they were seen, and which children were able to take care of their research tools (the checklist and crayon) by getting them back to school.

The second project was one in which we wanted to know how many vehicles were in the school parking lot [Figure 35 (right)]. Each child estimated the number. We took tally sheets out to the parking lot and, working in pairs, marked off the vehicles as we passed them. Again, I could see the teamwork and the ability to understand the concept just by looking through the papers.

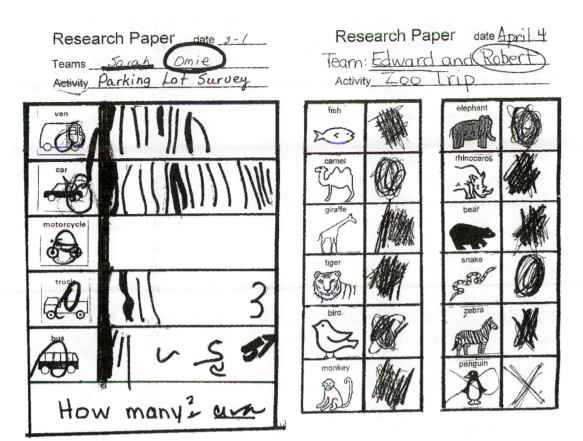

Figure 35. Research papers for a zoo trip and parking lot survey.

Note: Typically, children work in pairs, each with a different color crayon, so they can be distinguished when I review them. I usually draw a line with one color around the name of one child and use a different color and draw a line under the name of the other child. This way I know which child made which marks on the paper. Since this book is not in color, with reference to Figure 35, I had to distinguish Omie's and Sarah's work on the vehicle activity. In the case of Omie and Sarah, I traced over Omie's work (the numbers and lines she made) with a thicker pen to distinguish it from Sarah's. With Edward and Robert, I scribbled over Robert's work in a circular motion and over Edward's work in vertical fashion.

Notes and comments about their work

Information that forms the basis for my notes can often be gathered directly from the children when they are telling me about a picture, a drawing, a book, a building, a game, or any of the many activities in which children are engaged. I keep Post-it notes in my pocket, or nearby, just for that reason. When a child tells me about a painting, I jot down his words and stick the note on his work. Any comments he makes that give me more information about the child—his thinking, his attitude, and his perception—is worthy of adding to his portfolio.

In conclusion, any of the ideas and descriptions provided here for creating portfolios will help you document that children in your program are learning. To be sure you have descriptive and revealing portfolios for each child, collect work samples and write anecdotal recordings that:

- are consistent in what you collect
- can be stored in an orderly and retrievable manner
- are dated

Portfolios assemble the information that demonstrates to yourself, and to others, that children are learning, growing, and developing along an appropriate academic path.

In the next chapter we will discuss the anecdotal records. These are recordings you make about children's behavior, that is, what you *observe*. Before we move on, it is important that you know that anecdotal records are *brief*; and that they are *descriptions* of behavior, not *opinions* about behavior. Think about the difference as we turn to Chapter 4, Anecdotal Records.

Chapter 4

Anecdotal Records

"With her right hand, Ann drew large flowing loops and circles on her paper with a red marker. She colored each circle with a different color. As she changed colors she said a color word for each. She said for red, 'blue', for green, 'yellow', for blue, 'red.'"

An anecdote is a short story. Anecdotal records are slices of the lives of the children in your classroom. These records describe what a child does, but to be useful as measurement and assessment tools, anecdotal records must be factual, free of opinions, and non-judgmental. They must be accurate observations of what a child is doing written in a brief, narrative form.

Anecdotal records are statements about *behavior*. They record events that happen as children interact with their surroundings. Anecdotal records can be recorded during or after the event. Teachers use anecdotal records to gather information that is *not* collected by looking at samples of children's work. As with work sample collections, anecdotal records need to be written at regular intervals.

If you are trying to determine whether a child has obtained mastery of a skill on a developmental checklist such as "listens attentively to others," how do you decide? Since you cannot collect work samples that indicate the child is listening attentively, how would you document in your assessment that this developmental achievement has been accomplished by the child? The only way to get this information is to observe the child, and to record your observation just as soon as possible.

Many skills can be assessed in this way, so it is important that you develop a convenient and a simple way to observe and to record information about the children and their developmental progress. The recording method needs to be convenient and simple because it is part of your assessment continuum. Taking on new ways to document behavior is never easy. Like any new habit, in time and with practice it will become easier to master. The more often you use anecdotal records the more likely it is that you will continue to use them.

To observe children and to record those observations accurately, remember the following guidelines:

1. List the date, time, location, activity, and the name of the child on each recording.

Make sure that each observation has the date, the time, the location or activity, and the name of the child. The date is especially important when you look at growth over time. It tells you when he started working on a skill and when he mastered it. Your record establishes the baseline behavior from which all growth and change are measured.

2. Record only what you see.

Gather facts. Think of yourself as a video camera! Opinions, interpretations, and impressions such as these are to be avoided.

Elana __   October 11_   9:45 a.m. Woodworking Center

> Elana put one block of wood on top of another block. She understood measurement because she put a short nail beside the two blocks. It was not long enough to go through both blocks. She talked about the nail. She found a longer nail and figured it would go through both pieces of wood. She hammered the two pieces together. She was so proud of her work.

This record was filled with the teacher's opinions. Look at the *content* of the recording.

1. The teacher expressed his opinion that Elana understood measurement. This one observation does not reveal what she understood.
2. The teacher decided (for Elana) that her nail was not long enough to go through both blocks.
3. The teacher had no factual information that Elana figured out, on her own, that the shorter nail would not go through both blocks. In reading the record, we can only assume that Elana thought it.
4. Last, how do we really know that Elana was proud of her work?

For contrast, let's look at *factual, behavioral* statements about Elana's performance of the same activity.

Elana __   October 11_   9:45 a.m. Woodworking Center

> Elana put one block of wood on top of another block. She put a short nail beside the two blocks. She said, "This one is too short." She found a longer nail and put it beside the two blocks and said, "This will hold them together." Then, she hammered the two blocks together. She held it up and said, "Look! Look! I did it!"

This recording says the same thing as the first, but it excludes judgments and opinions. It is objective. The teacher can show a parent, and his principal for that matter, the recording. It is a factual observation about what Elana is learning about measurement.

Here are a few words that need to be *avoided* when recording observations:

he seems	he is trying	he appears	he wants
I think	it looks like	he avoids	he likes
he doesn't like	I believe	I feel	he can't
wrong	he meant	he understands	he feels

3. Include the child's own words.

Notice that by using the child's actual words the reader gains valuable information about what is going on. Analyzing the child's words later, after more information has accumulated, can provide valuable information about what the child is thinking. When you use the child's actual words in an anecdotal recording, put quotation marks around them so they can easily be identified as the child's. Write them exactly as the child says them.

4. Be positive.

As we discussed in Chapter 1, we want to look at what a child **can** do. Many things occur in the classroom, but most can be documented in a positive way, as long as, we document exactly what we **see**.

For example:

John ___ January 5_ 8:15 a.m. Arrival time

John ran into the classroom and threw himself down on the rug. His father walked away from the door to the classroom. John screamed, "Don't leave me! I hate school. You are mean!" John's father continued down the hall. John started to cry and ran to the door. He yelled, "Come back!" He laid down in the doorway and cried for five minutes.

Because this is written without opinions and impressions of John's behavior, it can be used along with other documentation of similar behavior to show that John is having difficulty adjusting to separation from his father. Perhaps some other interventions with John would be helpful. Since John was my student, I wanted to be prepared to document the basis for my concerns carefully. Direct observation, which describes John's behavior, is an accurate way to document his actions. Later, I used my assessment to justify my concerns with the parents and to create an individualized plan for John.

Obviously, in the example given above, one instance may not give you an accurate picture of John's problem. Several such incidents, occurring over time, suggest a pattern warranting other action. Anecdotal information can be shared with the parents to provide a constructive basis for an intervention or an individualized plan.

5. Be specific; record the events in the order that they happen, and give details.

This sounds simple and obvious enough, but details help us understand more about the environment. Details also give valuable information about what a child is learning. Better to say, for example, "William counted 1, 2, 3, 4, 6, 8, 9, 10" than to say, " William tried to count to 10." There is so much more information in the first example. Seeing the numbers he skipped helps us plan better for William and know where to go next with helping him learn to count in sequence.

6. Know what is important in what you are recording.

How do you know which details are important? Let's take another example. If you record that a child is looking at a book, turning the pages in order, and moving his finger along the printed text, what is the child's behavior telling you? Is it that he understands left-to-right, top-to-bottom progression? This is an important reading skill. It needs to be recorded. Anecdotal recordings are the best method for getting this kind of information into the child's portfolio.

Many teachers use developmental checklists or developmental report cards to keep track of the most important landmarks in a child's progress. I create a list of skills for every center in my classroom to help me know what is happening in each center (Figures 36 and 37) and post the lists at my eye level in each center so that I am reminded of what children are learning. Quickly, I can see the various skills that children develop there. The list helps me focus on a particular skill when I am taking anecdotal records and assures me that many skills overlap from center to center. Sometimes I am not sure of what I am seeing so the chart reminds me that she is learning matching, seriation, or one-to-one correspondence. Knowing what you are looking for, and accurately describing what you are seeing, helps make the recordings easier, faster, and more useful.

(A list for all the centers is in the back of the portfolio.)

7. Know how to use the information to look at one child's growth and change.

When we look at a compilation of anecdotal records on one child taken over time, we are gathering information about how the child is changing. That is the primary reason for writing the records. The series of anecdotal records that follows shows success for Tom. Tom is successful because he has grown and developed over time, not because he has achieved some performance standard established by others.

Children sit on carpet squares during group-time meetings in my class. At those times we work in group on concepts, group-project instructions, and on group tasks. One of the children's jobs upon first entering the classroom each day is to go to the group area where carpet squares define their personal sitting space. They pick up laminated sentence-strips, printed with their whole names, and they place them in a pocket chart located nearby. Then, they return to the same square where they find their name and they sit down. We call the sentence strips check-in cards.

Tom _____   October 2__   9:00 a.m.

In the Manipulative Center

Children learn to...

○ Match objects in a one-to-one correspondence
○ Orally identify the number of objects in a group
○ Recognize the empty set
○ Know terms related to direction and location
○ Use vocabulary to define quantities and relationships
○ Learn vocabulary to compare sets
○ Demonstrate concepts of part and whole
○ Compare objects
○ Form groups by sorting and matching
○ Combine and separate groups of objects to form new groups
○ Sort objects by one or more characteristics
○ Repeat a simple pattern using objects
○ Order two or three objects by size
○ Develop fine motor skills
○ Practice self-help skills
○ Develop pincher control
○ Develop perceptual awareness skills
○ Experience counting objects
○ Experience identifying patterns
○ Experience at the readiness level physical representations of addition and subtraction
○ Discover similarities and differences
○ Know the letters of the alphabet
○ Distinguish between upper and lower case letters
○ Sequence events correctly
○ Make predictions and explain why
○ Discover color, shape, line and texture
○ Explore money
○ Explore time units
○ Classify objects
○ Acquire eye-hand coordination
○ Make choices
○ Make decisions

Figure 36. List of skills for the Manipulative Center.

Group Time

Tom came into the room and looked at the carpet squares with the names on them. He held up Jason's name and asked, "Is this *my* name?" He held up Lana's name next, and again he asked, "Is *this* my name?" Sarah held up his name and gave it to him. He checked in.

The record above shows that Tom does not recognize the first letter of his name.

Tom _____   December 5__   9:00 a.m.
Group Time

Tom came in the room, looked at the names on the squares, got

---

In the Music Center

Children learn to...

○ Hear music for quiet listening
○ Hear music that tells a story
○ Create vocal sounds by imitating songs
○ Sing songs
○ Move and dance
○ Play a simple rhythm using musical instruments
○ Understand that music is a written language
○ Repeat a simple pattern with voice, movement or musical instrument
○ Create a pattern with musical instruments
○ Participate in rhythmic activities
○ Develop coordination
○ Acquire fundamental movement skills
○ Develop spatial and directional awareness
○ Recognize and compare sounds
○ Explore vocal sounds
○ Imitate and recognize environmental sounds
○ Explore differences in speaking and singing voices
○ Explore tone matching
○ Explore rote singing of melodic patterns
○ Recognize high/low, loud/soft, fast/slow, up/down and long/short
○ Hear short selections for expressive movement
○ Listen and identify simple music forms
○ Move to express mood/meaning of music
○ Move to express a steady beat
○ Explore singing games and action songs
○ Explore complicated rhythm patterns
○ Explore cause and effect, relationships, force, change and intensity
○ Make choices
○ Make decisions

Figure 37. List of Music Center skills.

Thomas' name and checked in. Thomas went and got Tom's name and gave it to Tom. Tom checked in again.

This record shows that while Tom recognized the first letter of his first name, he cannot recognize the other letters as his. Tom distinguishes "T" only.

Tom ___   February 22__   9:00 a.m. Group Time

Tom came into the room, got his name off his square and checked in. His square was next to Kevin's. He turned around from the check-in chart, and he looked at all the squares. He looked at the square next to Kevin, then at the one next to Ashley. He asked, "Where was my name?" No one responded. He sat on the square next to Ashley.

Now Tom recognizes his own name, but he does not remember where he got it!

Tom ____   April 2__   9:00 a.m. Group Time

Tom came into the room, went to the square with his name, picked up his name card, checked in, and returned to the square that had his name card on it originally.

Tom remembered not only his name, but which carpet square it was on.

Tom ____   May 15___   9:00 a.m. Group Time

Tom came into the room, went to his square, got his card, checked in, and read the other children's names on the check-in chart: "A.J., Sarah, Pancho, Kevin, Travis, and now Tom," he said. He returned to his square where his name originally was placed, and he said to Kevin, his neighbor, "You're sitting in the wrong place." Tom showed Kevin where Kevin's name had been before Kevin checked in.

Now, Tom is not only reading his own name, but the other children's names. He also recalled where not only he was supposed to sit, but where Kevin was supposed to sit as well.

In summary, what have we learned about Tom's growth and development from September through May? Let's look at just one area, reading and recall. Did he recognize his name in September? As we move through the records, and through time, we see that he:

1. Recognized the letter "T" at the beginning of his name and Thomas' by December 5.
2. Later learned to recognize his own name and location as well.
3. Learned to read the names of other children.
4. Initially could not remember where he got his name, but developed the recall as time progressed.
5. Later he learned his own name-location and then other children's locations as well.

Any one of these recordings would have told us very little about Tom's growth and change over time. We would have no appreciation for his progress. All of them together, however, gives us a more complete picture of his progress.

8. Know how to use the information you obtain from the child to guide curriculum planning.

Anecdotal records help us make immediate changes in the way we teach. They help us plan the next few moments, the next few days, and the next few weeks.

In my class, we planted pumpkin seeds in milk cartons and watched them sprout. The children were excited and were pleased with their gardening. In the Manipulative Center, I placed a set of sequence cards which took the children through six steps in the seed-planting, soil-watering, and plant-growing process. Most of the children were very successful with the cards. Tara, however, had a different experience. This is the anecdotal record I wrote about her experience.

Tara ____   October 20___   9:45 a.m. Manipulative Center
> **Tara chose the pumpkin sequence cards from the shelf. She placed the picture of the fully-grown pumpkin on the tray. She put the pumpkin seed picture next, and she moved the other sequence cards around on the tray. She pushed all of the sequence cards in the middle of the tray, and she put the tray back on the shelf.**

Watching Tara told me a lot about her growth and development. She had not moved-on from a hands-on, or real, frame of reference to a picture, or representational frame. In other words, accepting representations of things for the things themselves was a skill yet to be acquired by Tara. Perhaps, I thought, a six-sequence card set was just too many for Tara. Immediately, I put out a three-sequence set. She was still unable to put them in order.

I did more planning and decided she would be our class gardener for a while. She was to plant other seeds for the class and give us a daily update on the progress of the plants. The following week, she planted marigold, bean, and squash seeds. She watched them sprout from the soil and grow into plants. She reported to the class how the plants were doing. After three weeks, I observed Tara putting the six-sequence, pumpkin seed planting cards in order.

My observation of Tara, written in an anecdotal record, drove my planning for her. It also became a reference point for future work.

From this classroom example, you can see that a goal I had for the children was to sequence correctly cards depicting the six steps of a pumpkin seed planting and growing activity. I felt they were ready developmentally to move from the real to the representational. I had assessed the children, evaluated my plan, and found that for most children it was an attainable goal. With Tara, however, I needed to change my approach. I decided to first try a three-sequence set. When she was unable to do that, I assessed and evaluated again. Everyday I would model and walk through the real process with her. Tara would be the lead gardener and share her experiences in a class report. This made her feel good about herself, and drew attention away from what she could not yet do. She observed and reported over and over with the help of her teacher and her peers. After all of our efforts she was successful, not with the three-sequence set, but with the six-sequence set originally established as a goal for her.

9. Know how to use the information to evaluate your program.

With Tom and Tara, I used my observations and anecdotal records to evaluate the success of the learning experiences we provided in our classroom. Anecdotal records can be used to evaluate an entire program and its effectiveness with the children. By looking at the information provided by an *accumulation* of anecdotal records, such an evaluation is realistic and highly desirable.

Through anecdotal records kept on many children, I was able to recognize weaknesses and to change our math program. These records helped me determine that the current math program was not meeting the needs of the children in my classroom. The following records illustrate how they provided the necessary information for me to make changes.

Kerry _____   September 10__   9:30 a.m. Manipulative Center
> Kerry got the attribute blocks off the shelf. She dumped them onto the tray. She put a triangle with a circle and a square. She put a circle beside a rectangle. She stacked all the shapes on top of each other. When asked if she could find all the ones like this (a circle), she held up a triangle and a square.

Carl _____   September 10__   10:00 a.m. Manipulative Center
> Carl chose the shaped flannel-board figures. He put them on the flannel board. When he was asked if he could put the biggest ones together, he put a large triangle, a small triangle, and a small circle together.

Marisa _____   September 10__   9:45 a.m. Science Center

    Marisa chose the balance scale from the shelf. She selected crayons
to weigh on the scale. She placed three crayons on one side of the
scale, and one crayon on the other. She got 10 more crayons and
placed them on the side with one crayon. She looked at me and said,
"Why is this one (the left side of the balance scale) on the table?"
She pulled out all the crayons on that side. She said, "Mrs.
MacDonald, now it won't be the same!"

Kevin _____   October 26__   9:40 a.m. Manipulative Center

    Kevin chose the pattern-card activity. On the card he chose, there
were 2 red apples and 1 green apple in a pattern, repeated twice.
Following this pattern series, there were 3 uncolored apple silhou-
ettes. Kevin picked up a yellow apple and placed it on the first
silhouette; then, he put a red and green apple in the remaining two.

Robert _____   November 5__   8:30 a.m. Group Time

    After examining a tray of 7 apple seeds and 60 pumpkin seeds, I
asked Robert if there were more apple seeds or more pumpkin
seeds. Robert responded, "Apple!"

A.J. _____   November 20__   10:15 a.m. Snack Preparation

    A.J. was asked to hand the teacher 3 carrots. She handed her 6 of
them.

A.J. _____   November 29__   9:45 a.m. Science Center

    A.J. chose the pine cone seriation activity from the shelf. She put the
medium-size pine cone on the large pine cone silhouette; she put the
smallest pine cone on the medium silhouette. She pushed the large
pine cone around on the tray; then, she put it back in the basket. She
put the activity back on the shelf.

You can see from these records that the math activities I planned
were not meeting the needs of the children. Clearly they did not know
what to do with the activities. Over the Christmas holidays, I planned
a more in-depth math program. I was able to put it in place at the
beginning of the new year. Look at the anecdotal records you keep and
ask yourself:

- What specifically is this telling me about this child?
- What are the child's learning needs?
- What modifications in materials and activities do I need to make?
- Is there enough detail in the record to give me a clear picture of
  what this child does or doesn't understand?

Look for ways you can build what you learned in this book into your own setting. Using anecdotal records and work samples gives you an excellent portrait of each of your children.

Ways to Keep Anecdotal Records

Keeping track of anecdotal records is difficult. However, I have discovered a method that has made the job easier. I have a large chart on the wall behind the door to my classroom (Figure 38). Each child has a box on the chart. All of my anecdotal recordings are written on multicolored Post-it™ notes. I carry the pads and a pen in my pocket all of the time. As I observe the children, I write notes about their behavior and include the date, time, and the activity. Completed notes are stuck on the child's box on the chart. One glance at the chart lets me know which children have yet to be observed that week. I may use a pink notepad for the first part of the week and a yellow pad for the second part. At the end of each week, I pull off the notes and place them on a sheet of paper with the child's name at the top. I fold these and place them in the child's portfolio at the end.

These are other successful methods I have used or seen used by others for keeping the anecdotal records.

1. Write the recordings on index cards. File cards behind each child's name in a recipe box.
2. Divide a spiral notebook with tabs into sections for each child.
3. Write on large peel-off stickers. When one page of stickers is filled, peel them off and put them in a three-ring binder, with tabbed sections for each child.
4. Punch holes in the upper left-hand corner of two, blank index-cards for each child in the class and put them on notebook rings. When there are no blank index cards, you know you have two anecdotal records on each child. File cards by each child's name in a photograph box. Make a new ring every week.
5. Carry a clipboard around to write observations. File recordings at the end of the day in each child's folder.

Whatever method you choose, it needs to be quick and easy for you to record and to access later. The simpler the system the better. An elaborate method of anecdotal recording may tend to take you away from your most important job—facilitating, observing, teaching, and interacting with the children. Try different methods to see which method works best for you.

In conclusion, by collecting work samples and writing anecdotal records of what you are observing, you can begin to convince the schools and communities in which we work and live that we have a valid and reliable method for assessing the learning of young children. Properly set up and managed, young children's classrooms may initially look chaotic. The apparent lack of structure bothers some observers and other teachers who have not been exposed to the conceptual framework that underlies this method. The way young children learn, however, dictates an interactive hands-on approach.

The assessment methods outlined in this book provide evidence that young children are gaining a solid base of knowledge and skills. Portfolio assessment is a tool that reflects both the child's *and the teacher's* growth and change. It supports the thinking that goes on in the classroom, both from the child and from the teacher.

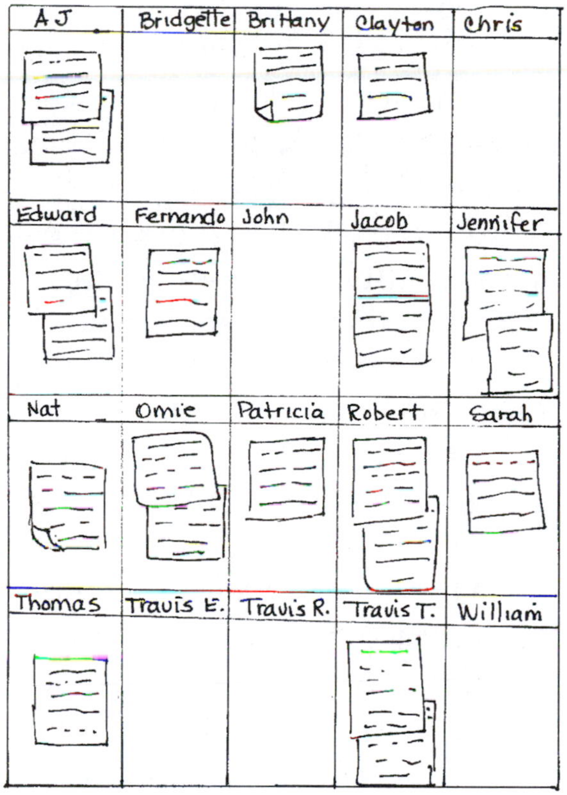

With these tools we are able to focus on what the children are doing, rather than what they are *not* doing. Such an assessment tool allows the children to learn and to progress at their own pace. Their progress is documented through work samples and through a variety of observed behavior that has been

Figure 38. Anecdotal Record Chart.

recorded over time in the form of anecdotal records. Portfolio assessment can either affirm the quality of an early childhood program or reveal shortcomings in it. It is the most effective and realistic tool for the assessment of young children that we have available.

Chapter 5

Using the Portfolio

"How do I know my child is going to be ready for the first grade? How do I know what my child is learning in school? What does my child need for me to help her with at home?"

Using Portfolios With Parents

Sometimes parents, as well as administrators might question the *effectiveness* of early childhood education and its methods. They may wonder if young children are learning the skills they need to successfully advance in their education. You need more than good answers, you need documentation.

Throughout the first four chapters of this book I have suggested that you use portfolios to assess young children. Parents, administrators, principals, and other teachers may need to become more familiar with portfolio assessment as a tool for measuring growth and change in young children in order to embrace it.

Questions about how we teach and why we do it that way makes us better teachers. We have discussed these three ideas earlier in this book:

1. assessment drives curriculum
2. curriculum drives activities and materials
3. children's experiences are modified (often immediately) by assessment that is taking place continuously

The interaction of curriculum and assessment creates a dynamic model of teaching that is very responsive to the needs of the individual child. Portfolio assessment also works well with children with special needs, as it focuses on strengths and progress, rather than weaknesses and failures. An excellent book that details the characteristics of children with special needs is found in *Children With Special Needs* (Leister, 1996).

Since parents are going to be the first to question these ideas, we want to get them involved in the assessment process when the school year begins. They need to know up front why their child's work is not graded with the numerical or "ABCDF" report cards. It is going to take time, patience, and education for the parents to understand and to accept the portfolio assessment model. We have much work to do to encourage them to value this method of evaluating their child. Remember if you make the parents a part of the evaluation team and keep accurate, well documented records, it will be much easier to address parental concerns as they happen.

I suggest that you start with a letter to families *in the fall* (Figure 39). Briefly introduce assessment and how the assessment process will unfold during the school year. The introduction letter, and the responses it has brought, have been helpful to me in establishing early, working relationships with parents. Use parts of it to create your own letter and add your own descriptions of what you will be doing in your classroom.

Another reason I like to have a fall conference with families is to show them a sample portfolio (on a child from a previous year with the name removed). From this example, they see the actual accumulation of work. It helps them see how their own child's progress can be measured and how growth and change are represented in the child's work. They come to understand the process and to reconcile the differences between their past experiences with report cards and grades when compared to portfolios. I

Dear Parents,

This letter is to introduce you to portfolio assessment. It is a different way of looking at your child's development. I will be collecting samples of your child's work during the year and making written notes about what I see your child doing. These will be the foundation of the portfolio that your child will build during the year.

We will include your child's stories, photographs, cutting activities, writing samples, paintings, and other things that give us information about how your child is learning, growing, and changing. I will make notes about how your child is playing with others, listening to stories, putting a story in order, working a puzzle, and showing how your child is learning to use his/her big and small muscles. As time goes on, we will collect many samples of different areas of learning to see how your child is developing in those areas.

There are many purposes of this way of assessing your child. One is to look at your child's growth over time in a natural setting based on real performance. So often a test only tells us what he or she could do on that day and that particular time. Portfolio assessment tells us much more. Another purpose of this type of assessment is that it increases the participation of your child in his or her own evaluation and focuses on what is "right" about your child. We want to look at what your child is doing, not what he or she is not doing. The last purpose of portfolio assessment is to help me as your child's teacher plan daily to meet his learning needs. The assessment will drive my instruction!

For this to work, I need your help. I will be sending home occasionally, a few samples of your child's work called a "showcase." I would like for your to share this with your child. It will help you see what your child is doing and help him celebrate his growth. Please feel free to add to your child's portfolio. If he or she does something you think would add to our knowledge of your child, please send it to school to be added to his portfolio.

I welcome your questions and comments.

Sincerely,

Your Child's Teacher

Figure 39. Introduction letter for the families.

can deal with their questions and their concerns, too, without having to refer to their own child's work (which sometimes has been a block to their initial understanding). They can view an unrelated child's work more objectively.

They can see, for example, how portfolio assessment presents a positive profile of a child. Along with the sample portfolio, they can see the child's baseline work samples. This will help them understand that their own child will be starting at some baseline level, gaining in skill and competence as she moves through the year. In this conference you can discuss with families common goals for *their* child. If their goals seem unrealistic (such as wanting a four-year-old to learn to read "The Three Billy Goats"), you can help reshape their expectations. Show them a continuum of reading development to help parents modify their view.

Include each child at the family's conference. It is *his* education that is being discussed, so his input is helpful, and establishes that children have a personal responsibility for their own learning.

New processes are often the source of many questions. You might suggest to the parents that they add to their child's portfolio by saving work samples from home, or by making notes about their child's activities and work at home. They can send them to school to be added to the child's portfolio. This will make them feel a part of the assessment process.

Another tool I use to educate the parents is the Portfolio Report illustrated in Figure 26. While the descriptive paragraphs beneath the pictures do not describe a particular child, *their* child for instance, the words help the parent understand in a general way how learning takes place in the classroom and how each center encourages children to learn necessary skills and concepts.

If you are using a developmental report card or checklist, explain to parents that you gather the information for the report card through the portfolio assessment process. In other words, you are extracting information from the portfolio about what the child is doing. Take time to explain the report card to parents so they will understand the progression of skills. This helps them look for and expect changes in their child.

Another method to help parents understand the portfolio process is to send home a "showcase" portfolio two or three times during the year. Showcase portfolio refers to pulling from the portfolio materials several examples of the child's work. The work is taken at different times during the year and sent home for the child to share with her family. These are returned to school the next day and replaced in the portfolio. You will need three examples of the child's work in a particular skill area to send home. For example, the first time (around February) you send home the showcase portfolio, include three paintings, three writing samples, and three math activities. The three examples from each category of work should be taken from different times periods sufficiently far apart in time to show the changes that have taken place. Showcasing the child's work in this way gets the parents used to comparing the child to herself, not to others.

Help the child choose the examples that show his growth and development and avoid excesses. Too much material sent home can be overwhelming to parents, and difficult for them to get through. What you want to do is to encourage them to celebrate their child's progress and his sense of accomplishment, without expecting him to measure up to some external standard. The joy the child feels about his accomplishments needs to be shared by the parents. In this way, both the parents and the child build self-esteem. It is also helpful in the education of the parents. The parents need to believe in the process if it is to be a permanent part of your program. Seeing the growth and change in their child, and understanding how the developmental continuum works, helps parents change their way of looking at assessment.

I like to have a spring conference, too, to look at the child's growth and change along her developmental path. Several days before the parents arrive, I review all the work samples and notes from the portfolio. I select the ones that show change in social-emotional, physical, aesthetic, and intellectual development.

Transitional pieces often are the most interesting in that they show the child working up to a seemingly insurmountable developmental barrier and then breaking through to a new level. When I find a child going beyond the old barriers, occupying new ground, these days are what make teaching worthwhile. Many times it is possible to share these moments with the parents by showing them several samples of work that record the breakthrough.

When I hold a parent conference, it is much like the example of a narrative on Casey that appears later in this chapter. I cover the same material and introduce work examples that support the narrative. I plan the conference carefully to avoid overwhelming families with too much information. I have learned to be extremely selective. I will show them <u>three</u> of each of the following:

- paintings
- writings
- photos of block constructions
- stories the child has written (or dictated)
- math work
- notes about social-emotional growth and physical changes

The whole portfolio is open for *them* to look at, but for the conference I focus on just a few main ideas. Reviewing the entire portfolio is *not* a good idea, not only because of time constraints, but because core ideas often get diluted by extraneous asides. It *is* a good idea to tell families what the accumulation of

Seeing the growth and change in their child, and understanding how the developmental continuum works, helps parents change their way of looking at assessment.

work tells about their child, where the child is on the developmental continuum, and how this will influence her experiences for the next year.

If you have a developmental report card, the information is pulled together for you. Explain to the parents that the teacher at the next level will pick up their child at the level where she stopped the previous year. It is much like a long airplane trip when the passenger stops at one airport, lays over for awhile, then boards another plane to continue the journey.

Passing On the Portfolio

At the end of the school year ask yourself, "Now that I have gathered all this information on children, what do I do with it?" It is a question that has several answers. What you do with the portfolio depends to a large extent on your school's policy. Storage is a very big issue, so you cannot save each portfolio in its entirety. On the following pages, we will look at several choices you have when considering what to do with your portfolios when all of the detail no longer is needed.

Pass the Portfolio to the Next Teacher

Some schools require that the portfolio information be passed on *in toto* to the next teacher or grade level. Developmental report cards or checklists are not used. If this describes the setting in which you find yourself, it is advisable to select the *most* significant work from the portfolio to pass on to the next teacher. As the school year comes to a close, select work samples that show the beginning, or "baseline" skill level, and the ending skill level. Start with writing, painting, math, dictated or written stories, and drawings. Also, include photos and plan book pages. You want to have a good cross-curriculum representation in what you select to send forward about the child. A teacher wants a comprehensive profile and a description of what a child has accomplished and, where-to-go-from-here ideas or recommendations about future instruction for the child. The remaining work in the portfolio needs to be sent home with the child.

Some school districts, for example, have the capability to scan, or capture, most of the portfolio information on CD ROM computer disks. In this form, the portfolio information can be passed along, from teacher to teacher, and virtually kept indefinitely.

Write A Narrative

Many schools require that teachers write a narrative that summarizes the information that has been collected in the portfolios over the previous school year. If you are required to do this, here are three suggestions about what the narrative should include:

1. What did the portfolio tell *you* about the child in each of the developmental domains: social-emotional, physical, cognitive, and aesthetic?

2. Where is the child on a developmental continuum?
3. What does the information tell you about the child's future learning needs? In other words, what do you suggest or recommend?

Along with a narrative, include a few samples of the child's work that confirm the growth and development in the areas you talk about in the narrative. The narrative does not need to be long or tedious. Just be concise, conveying the most significant information clearly. Your narrative needs to be a summary of the significant information accumulated in the portfolio during the school year. Let's look at a narrative that attempts to do just that.

Casey's Portfolio Narrative
August through May

Cognitive Development
Language Arts
Casey talks in seven- and eight-word sentences. She has started using themes in writing her stories. Casey tells long stories with a beginning, a middle, and an end. She uses initial consonant sounds frequently, and she sometimes adds vowels when writing, using invented spelling. She can sing a familiar song from start to finish. Casey can recount the sequence of the day's events. She repeats silly words often. Casey can describe simple cause-and-effect relationships. She identifies many letters of the alphabet and she understands position words such as *on, under, over* and *beside*. She has a 20-word sight-reading vocabulary. Reading to Casey is something that she enjoys. She listens attentively.

Casey is ready to begin work on:
- distinguishing words that begin with the same sound
- recognizing rhyming words
- recognizing more words in her environment

Mathematics
Casey can place five objects on the table upon request. She can count orally to 20, and she recognizes the written numerals 1 to 10. She recognizes circles, squares, triangles, rectangles, and ovals. Casey can place five objects in order by size if there are gross differences between the objects. She understands that time passes during the day.

Casey speaks of yesterday and tomorrow frequently. She understands one-to-one correspondence. Casey can create a pattern of two and she can repeat a pattern of three, with objects.

Casey is ready to:
- identify a cube, a sphere, and a cylinder
- work on identifying and naming an empty set such as zero
- work on creating patterns of three and four
- begin learning how to recognize sets of 6, 7, 8, and 9

Social and Emotional Development

Casey makes friends easily. She takes turns and shares when the occasion arises. She plays well with other children, and she negotiates for things she wants to have or to do. Casey demonstrates patience when waiting for her turn now, in immediate time and, she waits patiently to be group leader in the future, which might take weeks. Casey is willing to take risks with new experiences and people, and she will challenge the rules on occasion.

Casey is ready to work on:
- identifying expressions of feelings
- doing more work in teams or groups
- learning how to lead and how to follow in group settings
- solving challenging or difficult problems

Physical Development

Gross Motor: Casey uses her running skills to play games. She can gallop and jump smoothly and she can skip on one foot. She has mastered hopping. Casey can move toward a tossed ball and occasionally she catches it. She can toss a ball in the direction of a playmate. Casey can walk across the balance beam, forward or backward, with one foot in front of the other.

Casey is ready to master :
- skipping and jumping rope
- game-like situations with ball-tossing

Fine Motor: Casey can string large beads, lace a shape through large holes, and work a 10-piece puzzle. She can reproduce a circle, a line, a cross, and a square. She can cut along a straight line.

Casey is ready to:
- work with small beads and small parquetry blocks
- work with a 10- to 25-piece puzzle

77

- draw a triangle
- cut along a curved line

Aesthetic Development

Casey expresses her ideas through art projects. She has moved to the representational stage of painting, of drawing, and of block building. She goes to the easel with a plan in mind and she puts her plan on the paper. Casey participates in music and she initiates original songs. She enjoys using the puppets to dramatize original and familiar stories.

Casey is ready to :
- examine and replicate fine art
- create her own songs
- create her own puppet stories and characters

The natural progression of children's expansion of reading and art skills is shown in Figures 40 and 41. I use these benchmarks, and others like them, to help me determine where each child should be placed along a developmental continuum. This information helps me write the narrative.

Preparing a Developmental Report Card or Checklist

If you use a developmental report card, the information you gather during the year is used each reporting period as background documentation. The portfolio information helps you locate each child's developmental level along a continuum. The purpose of the portfolio is to help you gather this developmental information in a nonthreatening, familiar, and natural setting. This process can eliminate "sit-down testing" of children each reporting period. The information requested on the report card can be summarized from the portfolio materials to the report card. At the end of the year, you have a descriptive profile of what the child can do. I encourage you to keep a few pieces of each child's work as background data on which the report card information is based. The majority of the portfolio, however, needs to be sent home with the child at the end of the school year.

Conclusion

As you have seen from this discussion, the major uses of portfolios are to:

1. gather and convey information about a child's learning
2. inform families and keep them involved
3. transfer important information to children's future teachers

Much of how children's progress is evaluated will depend on your school's policy with respect to assessment. It is important to note, however, that portfolios can be used in most

---

Stages of Reading Development

Stage 1.   At this stage children: display an interest in handling books; see the construction of meaning from books as magical; listen to words read to them; play orally with letters or words; begin to notice print in an environmental context; sometimes incorporate letters in their drawings; and mishandle books, like "reading" them upside down (3 to 4 years old).

Stage 2.   At this stage children: engage in reading-like behaviors; try to magically impose meaning on new print; "read" contents of familiar story books; recognize their names; recognize words in environmental contexts; construct word meaning from pictorial clues; pick known words from print inconsistently; rhyme words; speak words that begin similarly; display an increasing knowledge of book handling; recall key words from poems and stories; and, they begin to internalize story grammar (4 and 5 years old).

Stage 3.   At this stage children can: write and read-back their own words; pick out individual words and letters; read familiar books or poems (that could not be repeated without the print); use picture clues to supplement print; read words in one context that may not be read in another; show increasing control over visual cueing system; enjoy chants and poems chorally read; detect the beginning/ending sounds in spoken words; blend phonemes; delete initial phonemes; recognize the letters of the alphabet; observe the differences between upper and lower case letters; and, match words in poems and chants that have been internalized (4, 5, and 6 year olds).

Figure 41. Stages of reading and development.

---

systems.

Portfolios can help you make decisions about children and how best to serve them. This approach is supported by knowledge that young children learn best in their natural surroundings and by interacting and experimenting with the adults, children, materials, and the ideas offered in an intriguing, engaging, prepared environment.

I wish you a pleasant journey through the portfolio process! Remember, the journey is just as important as the destination.

Stages of Art Development

Stage 1.   **SCRIBBLING:**   Children use crayons, markers and paint to in zigzag fashion and in circular motions. Later, the scribbles become more controlled. Their work is exploratory. Color is unrealistic. The child begins to draw symbols like circles, crosses and lines (3 and 4 year olds).

Stage 2.   **PRESCHEMATIC STAGE:**   At four, a child begins to show definite forms in representing a person, making a circle for the head and two vertical lines for legs. Sometimes there is a mouth, arms, hands, feet or shoes. Objects are drawn at random and they are not in sequence or proportion. At this stage, form is more important than color. As children progress through this stage size becomes more proportional, and they gain more brush control and their paintings begin to look more like illustrations. By age 7 a child has established a mental schema of an object that is repeated with each painted repetition of the object. For example, each time the child paints a house it will look very much like all the other houses she painted (4 to 7 years old).

Stage 3.   **SCHEMATIC:**   At this stage, sky lines (usually blue) and base lines (usually green) appear on the top and bottom of their drawings. Items drawn between these lines usually are proportional, and they are on the base line as appropriate (6 to 9 years old).

Source: Lowenfeld, V. (1954) <u>Your Child and His Art</u>. New York: MacMillan

Figure 40. Stages of art development.

References

Bredekamp, S. (Ed.) (1987). Developmentally appropriate practice in early childhood programs serving children from birth through age 8 (exp. ed.). Washington, DC: National Association for the Education of Young Children.

Grace, C., & Shores, E. (1994). The portfolio and its uses (3rd ed.). Little Rock: Southern Early Childhood Association.

Shores, E. (1995). Developmentally appropriate assessment. Worthington, OH: DLM/SRA.

For further reading

Barbour, N.H., & Seefeldt, C. (1993). Developmental continuity across preschool and primary grades: Implications for teachers. Wheaton, MD: Association for Childhood Education International.

Bredekamp, S., & Rosegrant, T. (Eds.) (1995). Reaching potentials: Transforming early childhood curriculum and assessment (Vol. 2). Washington, DC: National Association for the Education of Young Children.

Clemmons, J., Laase, L., Cooper, D., Areglado, N., & Dill, M. (1993). Portfolios in the classroom: A teacher's sourcebook. New York: Scholastic.

Darling-Hammond, L., Ancess, J., & Falk, B. (1996). Authentic assessment in action: Studies of schools and students at work. New York: Teachers College Press.

Drummond, M.J. (1995). Learning to see: Assessment through observation. York, ME: Stenhouse.

Jervis, K. (1996). Eyes on the child: Three portfolio stories. New York: Teachers College Press.

Koralek, D.G., Colker, L.J., & Dodge, D.T. (1993). The what, why, and how of high-quality early childhood education: A guide for on-site supervision. Washington, DC: National Association for the Education of Young Children.

Neill, M. (1996, Summer) What is the purpose of assessment? Rethinking Schools, 10 (4), 1, 12-13.

Neill, M., Bursh, P., Schaeffer, B., Thall, C., Yohe, M., & Zappardino, P. (1995). Implementing performance assessment: A guide to classroom, school and system reform. Cambridge, MA: FairTest.

Osten, M. (1996, Summer). Navigating the world of portfolios. Rethinking Schools, 10 (4), 14-15.

Paulson, F.L., Paulson, P.R., & Meyer, C.A. (1991). What makes a portfolio a portfolio? Educational Leadership, 48(5), 60-62.

Stone, S.J. (1995, Summer). Portfolios: Interactive and dynamic instructional tool. Childhood Education, 72(4), 232-234.

Stone, S.J. (1995). Understanding portfolio assessment: A guide for parents. Wheaton, MD: Association for Childhood Education International.

Woodward, H. (1994). Negotiated evaluation: Involving children and parents in the process. Portsmouth, NH: Heinemann.

Wortham, S.C. (1996). The integrated classroom: The assessment-curriculum link in early childhood education. Columbus, OH: Merrill.

Portfolio Forms

Table of Contents

Dear Parents,

This letter is to introduce you to portfolio assessment. It is a different way of looking at your child's development. I will be collecting samples of your child's work during the year and making written notes about what I see your child doing. These work samples and notes will be the foundation of the portfolio your child will build during the year.

Information about how your child is learning, growing and changing (such as stories, photographs, cutting activities, writing samples, and paintings) will be collected. Observations about how your child plays with others, listens to stories, puts a story in order, works a puzzle and uses large and small muscles will be added. As the school year goes on, we will collect many samples of different areas of learning to see how your child is developing.

This method of assessment will show your child's growth over time in a natural setting based on real performance. Often a test only tells what he or she could do on a particular day and at a particular time. Portfolio assessment also allows your child to participate in the evaluation. It focuses on what your child *is* doing rather than what he or she is *not* doing. Finally, portfolio assessment helps me as your child's teacher plan my instruction and to meet your child's individual learning needs. The assessment will drive my instruction!

Your help is important in assessing your child. Ocassionally, I will send home a few samples of your child's work called a "showcase". It will help you see what your child is doing. I would like for you to share and celebrate this with your child. Also, please feel free to add notes about activities and interactions that you observe to your child's portfolio. These notes will add to our knowledge of your child.

I welcome your questions and comments.

Sincerely,

Your Child's Teacher

1

Dear Parents,
Please help your child's teacher get to know him/her by filling out this form. All the information will be confidential and will be used only by your child's teacher in planning for his development. Please return it to school as soon as possible.
Thank you!

Child's name _____
                first   middle   last

Address _____

Nickname used by the family _____

Date of birth _____ Place of birth _____

Does your child live with: _____ both parents _____ one parent _____ other adults

  (please specify)_____

Names and ages of brothers _____

Names and ages of sisters _____

Pets (Name and type of animal)_____

Does your child have a room of his/her own? _____ If not, with whom does the

child share a room?_____

Which of these words best describes your child?

_____ lack self control   or   _____ uses self control

_____ independent   or   _____ dependent

_____ pleasant   or   _____ disagreeable

_____ attentive   or   _____ inattentive

_____ follow directions   or   _____ does not follow directions

_____ confident   or   _____ shy

In what ways is your child different from other children?_____

_____

_____

What are your child's favorite play activities and interests? _____

_____

What are your child's favorite T.V. programs?_____

How many hours a day does your child watch T.V.?_____

Does your child usually play ____ alone? ____ with one friend?

____ with many children? ____ with a few children? ____ with other children?

____ with younger children? ____ with children of the same age?

Is your child's play limited to the yard? _____ to the block? _____

Into how many homes does your child go frequently?_____

Is your child enrolled in any special group? _____

Has your child traveled out of town? _____ Where? _____

What are your child's responsibilities at home? _____

What does your child enjoy doing with the family? _____

How does your child get along with other children? _____

How does your child get along with other adults? _____

What is your biggest discipline problem? _____

_____

How do you discipline your child? _____

_____

How do you think your child will adjust to school? _____

_____

What fears does your child have? _____ animals _____ dark _____ storms

____ strangers ____ other _____

Does your child have any nervous habits? _____

Is your child right or left handed? _____

How does your child feel about going to school? _____

_____

What do you hope your child will learn this year? _____

_____

DAILY ACTIVITY CHART

Child's Name:_____ Date:_____ Recorder:_____

Check the box beside the time and place the child has chosen to work. This will track the child's movement and interest throughout the day.

WHERE THE CHILD IS WORKING

	B	A	M	H	S	W	C	PD	L	MS	WW	GM
7:30												
8:00												
8:30												
9:00												
9:30												
10:00												
10:30												
11:00												
11:30												
12:00												
12:30												
1:00												
1:30												
2:00												
2:30												
3:00												
3:30												

KEY:
B=Block   A=Art   PD=Play dough
H=Housekeeping   S=Science   MS=Music
M=Manipulatives W=Water Play   WW=Woodworking
L=Library   C=Construction   GM=Gross Motor

Parent Conference Notes

Name of parents:_____

Name of child:_____Date:_____

Name of teacher:_____

Things the teacher would like to share:

Things the parents would like to share:

Things the student would like to share (if present):

Specific goals agreed upon by all:

Stages of Art Development

Stage 1. Scribbling: Children use crayons, markers and paint in zigzag fashion and circular motions. Later, the scribbles become more controlled. Their work is exploratory. Color is unrealistic. The child begins to draw symbols like circles, crosses and lines (3 and 4 year olds).

Stage 2. Preschematic Stage: At four, a child begins to show definite forms in representing a person, making a circle for the head and two vertical lines for legs. Sometimes there is a mouth, arms, hands, feet or shoes. Objects are drawn at random and they are not in sequence or proportion. At this stage, form is more important than color. As children progress through this stage size becomes more proportional, and they gain more brush control as their paintings begin to look more like illustrations. By age seven a child has established a mental picture of an object that is repeated with each painted repetition of the object. For example, each time the child paints a house it will look very much like all the other houses he/she painted (4 to 7 years old).

Stage 3: Schematic: At this stage, sky lines (usually blue) and base lines (usually green) appear on the top and bottom of drawings. Items drawn between these lines usually are proportional, and they are on the base line as appropriate (6 to 9 years old).

Source: Lowenfeld, V. (1954) Your Child and His Art. New York: MacMillan

Stages of Block Play

Stage 1.   Tote and Carry: Blocks are carried around to feel their smoothness, their weight and to hear what kind of sounds they make when they fall. Children like to fill containers, dump them out, and refill them. (2 to 3)

Stage 2.   Building Begins: Children lay the blocks on the floor in rows, either horizontally or vertically with much repetition. Children may play alone or near other children, but rarely in a cooperative way. (3)

Stage 3.   Trial and Error Bridging: Two blocks with a space between them, connected by a third block. Children learn to bridge by trial and error. (3 to 4)

Stage 4.   Enclosures: Blocks are placed in such a way that they enclose a space. Bridging and enclosing are among the earliest "technical" building problems that children learn to solve. As children work at building enclosures, they learn the spatial concept of inside and outside. (4)

Stage 5.   Representational Building: At this stage, 4 and 5 year olds add dramatic play to their block building. They name their structures which relate to a function. Before this, children may also have named their structures but the names were not necessarily related to the function of the building.

Stage 6.   Building Sociodramas: By age 5, group cooperative play is common. Children decide beforehand what they want to build, and they may reproduce structures that are familiar to them. Children may ask to leave their structure standing and may play with it again.

Source: Hirsch, Elisabeth (1984) The Block Book. Washington, D.C.: NAEYC

Stages of Math Development

Stage 1.   Two and three year olds: begin to understand the use of numbers as they hear others using them; understand the use of numbers through exploring objects; work large-piece puzzles; understand direction and relational words; recognize geometric shapes, like a circle; and, sequence up to three items.

Stage 2.   Three and four year olds: recognize and express quantities like some, more, a lot, and another; begin to have a sense of time; recognize familiar geometric shapes in the environment; sort objects by one characteristic; rote count to 5; notice and compare similarities and differences; and use words to describe quantity, length, and size.

Stage 3.   Four and five year olds: play number games with understanding; count objects to 10 and sometimes to 20; identify the larger of two numbers; answer simple questions that require logic; recognize more complex patterns; position words; sort forms by shape; compare sizes of familiar objects not in sight; and work multi-piece puzzles.

Stage 4.   Five and six year olds: begin to understand concepts represented in symbolic form; can combine simple sets; begin to add small numbers in their heads; rote count to 100 with little confusion; count objects to 20 and more; understand that the number is a symbol that stands for a certain number of objects; classify objects by multiple attributes; and can decide which number comes before, or after, another number.

Stages of Motor Development

Three Year Olds: At this stage a child has difficulty with independent limb movement, shows wide flexibility in range of joints, walks with automatic gait, runs with increased smoothness, walks on a balance board, balances on one foot for an instant, alternates feet going upstairs, jumps off a low box with both feet together, throws an object with total body involvement, catches an object thrown directly into stiff outstretched arms, and shows readiness for riding a tricycle.

Four Year Olds: At this stage a child controls independent movement of body parts, shows increased spatial orientation, has a near adult style walking gait, shows increased smoothness when running, turns corners quickly, accelerates, decelerates and stops running motion, begins alternating feet while walking on a balance board, begins mastery of galloping skills, throws with arm only, relaxes arms as they move to catch an approaching object, and begins to control a bouncing ball.

Five Year Olds: At this stage a child shows increased control of fine movements, has increased endurance, uses running skills in play activities, has improved motion balance, has refined climbing skills, skips, gallops and jumps with smoothness, attempts to master hopping with increased sense of balance, shows rapid improvement in throwing skills, begins to move body to catch an object, begins to control a bouncing ball with one hand, shows increased leg backswing, follow-through and appropriate trunk rotation when kicking.

Stages of Oral Language Development

Stage 1.   Infant: A child at this stage smiles socially, imitates facial expressions, coos, cries, babbles, plays with sounds, develops intonation, and repeats syllables.

Stage 2.   18 months to two years: A child at this stage responds to specific songs, uses two-word sentences, depends on intonation and gesture, understands simple questions, and points and/or names objects in pictures.

Stage 3.   Two to three years: A child at this stage begins to use pronouns and prepositions, uses "no," remembers names of objects, and generalizes. There is a high interest in language and an increase in communication. There is a large jump in vocabulary growth and articulation.

Stage 4.   Three to four years: A child at this stage communicates needs, asks questions, begins to enjoy humor, has much better articulation, begins true conversation, responds to directional commands, knows parts of songs, can retell a story, speaks in three and four word sentences, is acquiring the rules of grammar and learns sophisticated words heard in adult conversation.

Stage 5.   Four and five years: A child at this stage has a tremendous vocabulary, uses irregular noun and verb forms, talks with adults on adult level in four to eight word sentences, giggles over nonsense words, engages in imaginative play using complex oral scripts, tells longer stories, recounts in sequence the day's events and uses silly and profane language to experiment and shock the listener.

Stages of Reading Development

Stage 1.   At this stage children display an interest in handling books; see the construction of meaning from books as magical; listen to words read to them; play orally with letters or words; begin to notice print in an environmental context; incorporates letters in their drawings; and mishandle books, like "reading" them upside down (3 to 4 years old).

Stage 2.   At this stage children engage in reading-like behaviors; try to magically impose meaning on new print; "read" contents of familiar story books; recognize their names; recognize words in environmental contexts; construct word meaning from pictorial clues; pick known words from print inconsistently; rhyme words; speak words that begin similarly; display an increasing knowledge of book handling; recall key words from poems and stories; and, they begin to internalize story grammar (4 and 5 years old).

Stage 3.   At this stage children can write and read-back their own words; pick out individual words and letters; read familiar books or poems (that could not be repeated without the print); use picture clues to supplement print; read words in one context that may not be read in another; show increasing control over visual cueing system; enjoy chants and poems chorally read; detect the beginning/ending sounds in spoken words; blend phonemes; delete initial phonemes; recognize the letters of the alphabet; observe the differences between upper and lower case letters; and, match words in poems and chants that have been internalized (4, 5, and 6 year olds).

Stages of Written Language Development

Stage 1.   Random Scribbling: Children make marks on paper randomly with little muscular control (2 and 3 year olds).

Stage 2.   Controlled Scribbling: Children "write" across the paper in linear fashion, repeating patterns over again, showing increased muscular control (3 year olds).

Stage 3.   Letter-Like Forms: Children make mock letters. These are written lines of letters that have letter characteristics but they are misshapen and written randomly, even covering the page. They like to pretend they are writing; and, in their work they separate writing from drawing. They have purpose to their letter-like forms (3 and 4 year olds).

Stage 4.   Letter and Symbol Relationship: Children write letters to represent words and syllables. They can write their name. They know the word that represents their name. They can copy words. Reversals are frequent (4 year olds).

Stage 5.   Invented Spelling: Children make the transition from letter forms to invented spelling. This requires organization of letters and words on the page. They use a group of letters to form a word.   Many of the letters will be consonants. They understand that letters relate to sounds. Some punctuation appears. They can copy words from their environment (4 and 5 year olds).

Stage 6.   Standard Spelling: Most of the words the children use are written correctly, some add punctuation. They organize their words in lines with spaces between the words; and, they move from left to right, and from the top of the page to the bottom (5, 6 and 7 year olds).

Stages of Social Development

Stage 1.   At this stage children wander around and watch others play. They do not participate or talk to the others playing.

Stage 2.   At this stage children watch others play, ask questions and make suggestions but do not participate. They are likely to leave if asked to interact.

Stage 3.   At this stage children play alone. They might act out a role alone with no apparent awareness of others. They select a toy with which to play but show no interest in other children's activities.

Stage 4.   At this stage children play near other children and may play with the same objects but they do not interact with the other children. The children play side by side and at times they might make conversation with themselves but not with the other children in the same area.

Stage 5.   At this stage children play with each other; are engaged in activities; and they may exclude some children. They rarely negotiate about the direction of their play. They interact with others at various times to share props, or, to have a partner in play.

Stage 6.   At this stage children organize their play, assigning roles, and negotiating turns. There is constant chatter about the roles the children are playing. They recognize the benefits of working together. They are able to share the materials and take turns using them.

In the Art Center

Children learn to ...

☐ Discover line, color, shape and texture by seeing and feeling objects

☐ Experiment informally with a variety of simple media

☐ Express individual thoughts and feelings through picture making, modeling, constructing and printing

☐ Look at and talk about artworks including primary sources

☐ Engage in conversation by sharing ideas with others

☐ Use the senses to gain information about the environment

☐ Develop problem solving skills

☐ Develop independence

☐ Develop organizational skills

☐ Experiment with art materials to understand properties

☐ Experiment with art materials to understand cause and effect

☐ Explore artwork

☐ Develop manipulative skills

☐ Develop eye-hand coordination

☐ Respond to story telling by drawing or painting

☐ Observe color, texture, size and shape of objects

☐ Make choices

☐ Make decisions

In the Block Center

Children learn to...

- [ ] Use oral language in a variety of situations
- [ ] Match objects in a one-to-one correspondence
- [ ] Learn social skills appropriate to group behavior
- [ ] Use vocabulary to designate quantities
- [ ] Use vocabulary to designate relationships
- [ ] Demonstrate concepts of part/whole
- [ ] Use vocabulary to compare objects (same/different)
- [ ] Form groups by sorting and matching objects according to their attributes
- [ ] Know and discuss the consequences of actions in social relationships
- [ ] Acquire nonlocomotor movement skills
- [ ] Create, repeat and/or extend patterns
- [ ] Develop eye-hand coordination
- [ ] Observe and follow safety rules
- [ ] Learn ordering
- [ ] Learn mapping skills
- [ ] Learn physical representations of addition and subtraction
- [ ] Develop classification skills
- [ ] Learn size and shape differentiation, relations and recognition
- [ ] Discuss ways people help each other
- [ ] Express relative sizes
- [ ] Understand gravity, stability, weight and balance
- [ ] Think, create and implement plans
- [ ] Discover properties of matter
- [ ] Discover the names of buildings and the functions of buildings
- [ ] Develop respect for the work of others
- [ ] Make choices
- [ ] Make decisions

In the Computer Center

Children learn computer skills. They learn to...

- [ ] Watch the screen
- [ ] Move the arrow to a specified place using the track ball or mouse
- [ ] Match letters using the track ball or mouse
- [ ] Use the keyboard to access the screen
- [ ] Match letters using the keyboard
- [ ] Draw with the mouse or track ball
- [ ] Fill in spaces with the track ball or mouse
- [ ] Erase with the track ball or mouse
- [ ] Choose activities using the program menu
- [ ] Use a menu to access a different program of choice
- [ ] Use the keyboard to write letters, words or numbers
- [ ] Print out a page

Children learn skills and concepts depending on the software.
They learn to...

- [ ] Match objects in one-to-one correspondence
- [ ] Match letters
- [ ] Compare objects
- [ ] Recognize similarities and differences
- [ ] Count objects
- [ ] Match pairs, sort and classify objects
- [ ] Discover color, line, size and shape of objects
- [ ] Combine sets
- [ ] Identify or repeat a simple pattern
- [ ] Extend or create a simple pattern
- [ ] Demonstrate the concept of part/whole relationship
- [ ] Develop perceptual awareness skills
- [ ] Know terms related to direction
- [ ] Recognize the printout is the same as the screen

In the Construction Center

Children learn to...

- ☐   Develop fine motor skills
- ☐   Express themselves through construction materials
- ☐   Repeat a simple pattern
- ☐   Develop perceptual awareness
- ☐   Develop pincher control
- ☐   Participate in cooperative play
- ☐   Express individual thoughts and feelings through constructions
- ☐   Experiment informally with a variety of simple materials
- ☐   Acquire the meaning of vocabulary words relating to concepts
- ☐   Make choices
- ☐   Make decisions

In the Dramatic Play Center

Children learn to...

☐ Use a variety of words to express feelings and ideas

☐ Use oral language in a variety of situations

☐ Match objects in a one-to-one correspondence

☐ Learn social skills appropriate to group behavior

☐ Identify basic economic wants of people

☐ Explore different celebrations and customs

☐ Know and observe rules of the classroom

☐ Explore sequences in basic family routines

☐ Experience consequences of actions in social relationships

☐ Practice self-help skills

☐ Participate in leadership/followship roles

☐ Develop concept of family by practicing roles

☐ Work cooperatively

☐ Practice simple home chores

☐ Engage in creative dramatic activities

☐ Engage in nonverbal communication

☐ Speak clearly and at an appropriate rate

☐ Engage in one on one communication

☐ Discover ways people help each other

☐ Discover socially acceptable and unacceptable behavior

☐ Discover cause and effect, interaction of materials and change

☐ Match pairs, sort and classify objects

☐ Share materials and take turns

☐ Make choices

☐ Make decisions

In the Gross Motor Center

Children learn to...

- ☐ Develop muscular strength and endurance
- ☐ Develop flexibility and cardiorespiratory endurance
- ☐ Develop locomotor skills
- ☐ Develop nonlocomotor skills
- ☐ Manipulate bean bags, large balls, long ropes, and hoops
- ☐ Perform body mechanics
- ☐ Develop body awareness
- ☐ Develop spatial and directional awareness
- ☐ Develop coordination and balance
- ☐ Participate in cooperative games
- ☐ Develop and practice behavior reflective of good sportsmanship
- ☐ Develop and practice behavior that reflects an understanding of safety
- ☐ Develop primary gymnastic skills (crawling, rolling, creeping, scooting, sliding and balancing)
- ☐ Respect equipment and materials
- ☐ Make choices
- ☐ Make decisions

In the Library Center

Children learn to .....

- ☐ Respond to simple directions, commands and questions
- ☐ Recognize and compare familiar and unfamiliar sounds
- ☐ Acquire the meaning of vocabulary works
- ☐ Listen to literary selections for personal enjoyment
- ☐ Use a variety of words to express feelings and ideas
- ☐ Dictate ideas and feeling as they are recorded
- ☐ Retell a familiar story
- ☐ Use oral language in a variety of situations
- ☐ Read own stories to others
- ☐ Create stories using invented spelling
- ☐ Develop fine motor skills
- ☐ Identify author and illustrator as being creators of stories
- ☐ Focus attention on a teacher
- ☐ Listen to appreciate sound devices of rhythm, rhyme, alliteration and onomatopoeia
- ☐ Relate events from personal experiences
- ☐ Communicate effectively in one-on-one and small group situations
- ☐ Tell what a story is about
- ☐ Recall important facts from a story
- ☐ Arrange the events of a story in sequential order
- ☐ Distinguish between real and make-believe
- ☐ Retell an unfamiliar story
- ☐ Respond to various forms of literature
- ☐ Become acquainted with a variety of selections, characters and theme of our literary heritage
- ☐ Select books for individual needs and interests
- ☐ Follow simple story lines in stories read aloud
- ☐ Recognize that everyone has experiences to write about
- ☐ Recognize that writing can entertain and inform

In the Manipulative Center

Children learn to...

- ☐ Match objects in a one-to-one correspondence
- ☐ Orally identify the number of objects in a group
- ☐ Recognize the empty set
- ☐ Know terms related to direction and location
- ☐ Use vocabulary to define quantities and relationships
- ☐ Learn vocabulary to compare sets
- ☐ Demonstrate concepts of part and whole
- ☐ Compare objects
- ☐ Form groups by sorting and matching
- ☐ Combine and separate groups of objects to form new groups
- ☐ Sort objects by one or more characteristics
- ☐ Repeat a simple pattern using objects
- ☐ Order two or three objects by size
- ☐ Develop fine motor skills
- ☐ Practice self-help skills
- ☐ Develop pincher control
- ☐ Develop perceptual awareness skills
- ☐ Experience counting objects
- ☐ Experience identifying patterns
- ☐ Experience at the readiness level physical representations of addition and subtraction
- ☐ Discover similarities and differences
- ☐ Know the letters of the alphabet
- ☐ Distinguish between upper and lower case letters
- ☐ Sequence events correctly
- ☐ Make predictions and explain why
- ☐ Discover color, shape, line and texture
- ☐ Explore money
- ☐ Explore time units
- ☐ Classify objects
- ☐ Acquire eye-hand coordination
- ☐ Make choices
- ☐ Make decisions

In the Music Center

Children learn to.....

- ☐ Hear music for quiet listening
- ☐ Hear music that tells a story
- ☐ Create vocal sounds by imitating sing songs
- ☐ Move and dance
- ☐ Play simple rhythm using musical instruments
- ☐ Repeat simple patterns with voice, movement and/or musical instruments
- ☐ Participate in rhythmic activities
- ☐ Develop coordination
- ☐ Acquire fundamental movement skills
- ☐ Develop spatial and directional awareness
- ☐ Recognize and compare sounds
- ☐ Formulate patterns
- ☐ Explore vocal sounds
- ☐ Explore imitation/recognition of environmental sounds
- ☐ Explore difference between speaking and singing voices
- ☐ Explore tone matching
- ☐ Explore rote singing of melodic patterns
- ☐ Sing action songs
- ☐ Recognize high/low, loud/soft, fast/slow, up/down, long/short, and smooth/jerky
- ☐ Hear short selections for expressive movement
- ☐ Listen and identify simple music forms
- ☐ Perform gross motor movement to records and singing
- ☐ Move to express mood/meaning of music
- ☐ Move to express steady beat and body sounds
- ☐ Explore sounds
- ☐ Explore singing games
- ☐ Explore complicated rhythm patterns
- ☐ Make choices
- ☐ Make decisions

In the Playdough Center

Children learn to...

- ☐ Use their senses to gain information about the environment
- ☐ Compare and contrast textures
- ☐ Use vocabulary to designate quantities such as: more than; less than; equal to; and, as many as
- ☐ Demonstrate concepts of part and whole with manipulative materials
- ☐ Acquire fundamental movement skills
- ☐ Develop fine motor skills like pincher control
- ☐ Develop perceptual awareness skills such as coordination
- ☐ Discover properties of matter
- ☐ Express self creatively
- ☐ Discover cause and effect, model, interaction of materials, and change
- ☐ Use tools to help
- ☐ Combine objects
- ☐ Compare similarities and differences
- ☐ Use vocabulary such as hard/soft, fat/thin, long/short, and in/out
- ☐ Work cooperatively
- ☐ Share materials
- ☐ Make choices
- ☐ Make decisions

In the Pouring Center

Children learn to...

- ☐   Recognize the empty set
- ☐   Know terms related to direction and location
- ☐   Compare and contrast similarities and differences
- ☐   Use vocabulary to designate quantities such as: more than; less than; equal to; and, as much as
- ☐   Use senses such as taste, smell, touch, sight and sound
- ☐   Acquire fundamental movement skills
- ☐   Practice self-help skills
- ☐   Develop pincher control
- ☐   Develop perceptual awareness skills
- ☐   Understand gravity, stability, weight and balance
- ☐   Explore force, cause and effect, and systems
- ☐   Discover properties of matter
- ☐   Develop awareness of cycle, interaction of materials, and change
- ☐   Understand volume and measurement
- ☐   Observe relationships between materials
- ☐   Make choices
- ☐   Make decisions

In the Woodworking Center

Children learn to...

- ☐ Identify basic economic wants of people
- ☐ Know and observe rules of the home, classroom and school
- ☐ Discuss what families do together
- ☐ Use the senses to gaining information about the environment
- ☐ Develop fine motor skills
- ☐ Develop pincher control
- ☐ Develop spatial and directional awareness skills
- ☐ Develop coordination
- ☐ Develop a healthy self-concept
- ☐ Develop creative expression
- ☐ Develop a willingness to try again
- ☐ Develop pride in work
- ☐ Develop a willingness to try new things
- ☐ Explore force, cause and effect, and properties of the materials
- ☐ Develop safety awareness
- ☐ Understand stability and balance
- ☐ Work independently
- ☐ Develop flexible, fluent, and unique thinking
- ☐ Work with measurement tools
- ☐ Explore relationships and interaction of materials
- ☐ Make choices
- ☐ Make decisions

In the Science Center

Children learn to...

☐ Use senses to gain information about the environment

☐ Describe phenomena in the environment

☐ Use vocabulary to compare objects

☐ Compare similarities and differences among objects

☐ Sort objects from the environment according to one or more characteristics

☐ Sequence events in order of their occurrence

☐ Know and practice safety

☐ Talk about what is seen, heard, touched, tasted or smelled as objects, people and events are experienced

☐ Use comparators

☐ Observe color, texture, size and shape of objects

☐ Observe change in the environment and objects in it

☐ Observe cause and effect of materials

☐ Observe systems, cycles, interactions and diversity in the environment

☐ Classify objects from the environment as living or nonliving

☐ Describe external features of organisms

☐ Make predictions

☐ Use the scientific method

☐ Develop curiosity about the natural world

☐ Observe relationships between objects

☐ Use weighting and other measurement skills to gain information

☐ Observe forces, such as gravity and magnetism

☐ Respect and use tools appropriately and safely

☐ Match, sort and classify objects

☐ Group objects

☐ Make choices

☐ Make decisions

PORTFOLIO REPORT

Child's Name:_____

Date:_____

Learning Center:_____

(Place photo or sample of child's work here.)

TEACHER COMMENTS:

_____

_____

_____

_____

_____

PORTFOLIO REPORT

Child's Name: _Janie Doe_

Date: _8/5/95_

Learning Center: _Outdoors_

(Photo of child on playground)

TEACHER COMMENTS:

Janie used words to express her anger when the tricycle was taken away from her.

SAMPLE TEACHER COMMENTS
FOR PORTFOLIO REPORTS

FOR THE ART CENTER:

The Art Center is an exciting place for children to work. It draws them like a magnet.   Children come to the center, choose an activity, and work that activity independently. They use the rebus (directions printed in picture form) that accompanies the activity as their guide. This gives them an opportunity to begin work immediately without waiting for directions. It also becomes a reading tool as they must "read" the directions before beginning to work. When children cut with the scissors, they use those small muscles to do what the eyes tell them to do. Lots of practice using fine muscles is needed before children make precise marks on paper. As children learn to use the art media to express themselves, they develop the ability to think creatively and solve problems.

FOR A PAINTING ACTIVITY:

When children work in the Art Center they are learning more than how to paint. They are learning reading, writing and math. Reading occurs when children see the differences in their strokes and learn to duplicate different strokes or shapes. Recognition of likenesses and differences are basic skills necessary when learning to write and do math. When children use thin and thick brushes or paint thin and thick lines they are learning math. Math skills also evolve when children select and paint on paper of different shapes . When children try to title their painting or put their names on the paper they are practicing writing skills. Skills that are the foundation of writing such as learning about spacing things on paper, working from the top to the bottom, and painting from the left to the right develop when a child is in the Art Center. Creativity blossoms when children are painting. There are many ways to put the paint on the paper and many ways to express ideas and thoughts. Expressing creativity leads to building problem solving skills.

FOR A PLAYDOUGH ACTIVITY:

Working with playdough offers children opportunities to explore different textures. Children roll, pinch, squeeze, pound, and bend the dough creating different shapes and objects. These activities give them the opportunity to expand their math skills by working with different amounts of playdough, creating shapes, and cutting it into fractions. Through playdough work children develop fine muscles that will help them later with writing skills. Using cookie cutters and rolling pins add another dimension to the Playdough Center. Children have the opportunity to work with a friend and share ideas and tools.

FOR OUTDOOR ACTIVITIES:

As children play outdoors they are developing control over their bodies and movements. They are learning how their body parts interact and how to make one side do what the other side can do. This coordination of both sides of the body is called integration. Running, jumping, throwing a ball, sliding, riding a tricycle are fun ways children develop coordination of both large and small muscle skills. Outdoor play gives children opportunities to use whole arm movement and leg muscles. These activities are essential to physical development and help in the development of the small muscles needed for precise tasks. Reading, math and writing develop when children have control of their bodies and their muscles. Finally outdoor play, gives children an opportunity to work on social skills in a less restricted environment. In an outdoor setting children learn to share, take turns, express hurt feelings, and work cooperatively with peers.

FOR THE LIBRARY CENTER:

The Library Center is the heart of the classroom. Here the children have opportunities to write stories, read stories, listen to stories on the tape recorder, and write letters. Children also have the opportunity to share these activities with their friends. Imagine how rewarding it is when one child writes a letter, "mails" it to a friend, and his or her friend reads the letter. Reading, writing, listening, and language development happen in this center. Children learn to enjoy and appreciate good literature as they explore their own creative efforts. Taking care of books becomes a part of a routine as children understand the value of books and develop a love of reading that will last a lifetime.

FOR THE BLOCK CENTER:

The Block Center is a very versatile learning place. Reading, writing, math, language, and social skills occur through the use of blocks. When children plan and organize their structures they are learning beginning skills necessary for reading and writing. Children develop important thinking skills such as creating balance, order, and symmetry as they work with blocks. Blocks are in direct mathematical proportion so fractions, part/whole relationships, shapes, and counting are a natural part of building. When children work together to create a structure, they are sharing not only the blocks but their ideas and plans for the structure. Planning together gives them a reason to work cooperatively.

FOR THE WOODWORKING CENTER:

The Woodworking Center is a source of pleasure for young children. As children use adult tools with care and respect, they learn to be responsible and trustworthy. Many math skills are learned in the center such as one to one correspondence, fractions, measuring and counting. Creative thinking and problem solving is developed when children have a short nail and two thick wood pieces to be nailed together. Children build self esteem as they feel competent in their woodworking, and master driving a nail into a block of wood.

30

FOR THE POURING CENTER:

The Pouring Center is a place to learn many different concepts and skills. Children learn math by measuring volume, weight, balance and distance. In addition, they learn the concepts of more and less, empty and full, and solid and liquid. They develop fine motor skills when they scoop, pour, drip, dump and mix. Children develop scientific principles when they explore different textures and experiment with the properties of many kinds of materials. Vocabulary is increased as children work with and talk about the funnels, water wheels, basters, and pipettes. As they move wet sand they "excavate" and when they make a channel for the water to move through they construct a "canal" and sometimes they make a "dam" to stop the water from moving.

FOR THE CONSTRUCTION CENTER:

The Construction Center is a favorite place because all the activities are open-ended since the toys have no stopping point. By having open-ended materials, children can develop the ability of take different approaches to solve problems they encounter while building. There are no wrong" or "right" answers at this center. The children play with small connecting blocks, toys with various shapes, logs for cabin building and similar toys. When the children are creating a pattern, putting pieces together to form a whole, or measuring their construction they are using math skills. The purpose of the Construction Center is not to have a "finished product" but to give children the opportunity to experiment, initiate, create, and solve problems.

FOR THE MANIPULATIVES CENTER:

The Manipulatives Center has many different areas such as a flannelboard, a magnet board, a puzzle shelf, and games. There are many choices so that children have many opportunities to select an activity of interest to them. At this center your child works a puzzle with a friend or learns to share cooperatively by playing a game. Finding the different pieces of a puzzle helps your child learn about similarities and differences or figure ground perception (distinguishing shapes from their background). Puzzle work also helps develop the understanding of the part/ whole relationship, a valuable math and reading skill. By working with a friend there are lots of opportunities to negotiate and problem solve which leads to the development of effective communication skills.

FOR THE SCIENCE CENTER:

The Science Center provides children with opportunities to explore their environment as they learn and explore cause and effect, cycles in nature, comparisons, chemical and physical changes and the properties of matter. Through simple activities children build a foundation for future scientific learning. As curiosity builds, children learn to be patient with projects that take time and how to make decisions based on data they gather. A basic skill for "scientific research" is the ability to see how things are the same and how they are different. Developing the ability to understand likenesses and differences builds a science base as well as a skill basic to reading and math.

FOR THE DRAMATIC PLAY CENTER:

As children play in the Dramatic Play Center, they learn to take turns, share, and select their friends based on common interests. They take on family and community roles that help them understand what other people do and how they act. In essence children have an opportunity to try on a role to see if it fits their personality style. The Dramatic Play Center helps them learn to make choices and decisions as they discover ways people help each other. Both math and reading skills are practiced as the children use a variety of objects like the phone book, recipe book, coupons, and a guide to television programming. Children learn to problem solve, work out difficult situations, develop vocabulary and practice social interaction in the Dramatic Play Center.

FOR THE MUSIC CENTER:

Children are naturally drawn to the Music Center. As children sing songs or move to the beat of the music, they explore and practice important developmental skills. Singing helps children develop new vocabulary words, practice words they already know, create and imitate sounds, recognize and repeat patterns, and compare sounds to each other. Science skills also develop as children strike a triangle and discover cause and effect. They learn about pitch, volume, and sound waves. Large muscles are developed as children express the mood of what they hear with their body movements. Movement, music and children go hand-in-hand.

FOR COMPUTER ACTIVITIES:

As children use the computer they begin to feel comfortable with technology and to understand its capabilities. They are developing a critical foundation to build on and add to all through school. Computer use is an everyday choice for the children as it becomes another "play" activity. Software is the key to using the computer as an effective learning tool. Through appropriate software children can solve meaningful, real-life problems, express themselves in writing and drawing, experience math problems, and discover solutions.

Rating Scale

Child's Name_____

Key: 1 - needs more time
2 - satisfactory
3 - excellent

Behavior:		Date	Rate
Comments			

Rating Scale

Child's Name_____

Key: 1 - needs more time
2 - satisfactory
3 - excellent

Behavior:		Date	Rate
Comments			

Computer Skills Checklist

Name _____

+ signifies that the child can do the task
− signifies that the child cannot do the task

	baseline 1	update 2	update 3	update 4	update 5	update 6
DATE						
watches screen						
uses track ball or mouse to move arrow						
moves arrow to specified place using track ball or mouse						
matches letters using the trackball or mouse						
uses keyboard to access the screen						
matches letters using the keyboard						
draws with the mouse or trackball						
fills in spaces with the mouse or trackball						
erases with the mouse or trackball						
chooses activity using program menu						
uses menu to access program of choice						
uses keyboard to write letters, words, or numbers						
matches the printout with the screen						

Checklist created by Virginia Fleury and Sharon MacDonald

Reading Log

Title	Liked	Did Not Like
	🙂	🙁
	🙂	🙁
	🙂	🙁
	🙂	🙁
	🙂	🙁
	🙂	🙁
	🙂	🙁
	🙂	🙁

Research Paper

Teams _____

Activity _____

date _____

Research Paper

Teams _____

Activity _____

date _____